A
MOORLAND
YEAR

HOPE L. BOURNE

Hope L. Bourne

EXMOOR BOOKS

Hope L. Bourne
First published 1993

EXMOOR BOOKS
Dulverton, Somerset

Trade sales enquiries:
Westcountry Books
Chinon Court
Lower Moor Way
Tiverton. EX16 6SS
Tel: 0884 243242
Fax: 0884 243325

Exmoor Books is a partnership between
The Exmoor Press and Exmoor National Park

British Library Cataloguing in Publication Data
A CIP Catalogue Record for this book is
available from The British Library

ISBN 0 86183 253 1

Designed for Exmoor Books by
Topics Visual Information
397 Topsham Road
Exeter EX2 6HD
0392 876800

Printed in Great Britain by Bookcraft, Midsomer Norton

C O N T E N T S

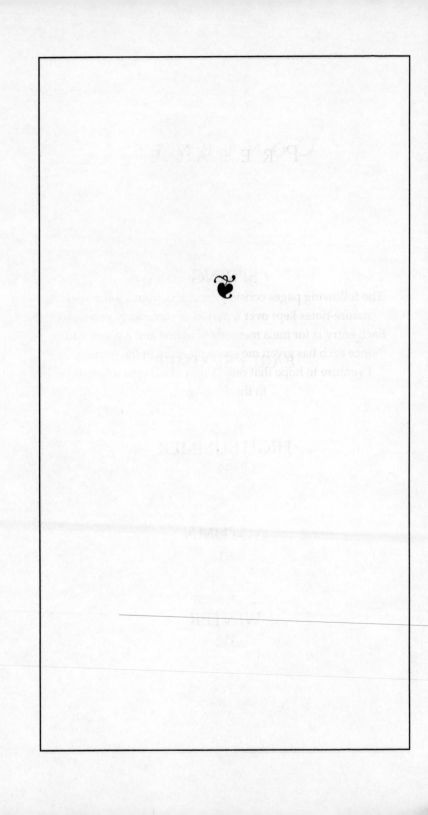

PREFACE

The following pages consist of extracts from a journal of
nature-notes kept over a period of some forty years.
Each entry is for me a memory of a time and a place, and
since each has given me some pleasure in the writing,
I venture to hope that others may find some interest
in the reading.

H.L.B.

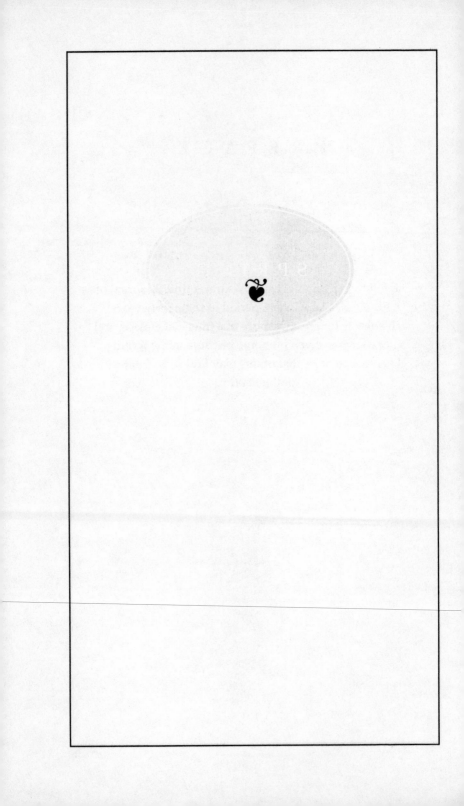

SPRING

In the valley under the moor the snowdrops carpet the floor and fleck the hillsides with their whiteness. Amongst the moss and crumpled fern and drifts of leaves and old sear grass, under the dark and dripping trees and bare black branches they raise their delicate heads from the earth in proclamation of the spring. For Candlemas Day has come and gone, and the Fair Maids of February grace the valley again with the promise that winter is passing, that cold and the short bitter days will not last for ever, and sunshine and warmth will return to the land.

Even now a soft brightness of sunlight descends from a slight rift in the grey cloud and touches the little water-falls of the threading stream to flashing silver. I stand for a while, and feel the stirring of life in all things.

Here is the door to Paradise, the hope of summer, but high above on the hills winter still reigns and rules, and will do so for perhaps three more months. Black wet heather, sodden dun moor-grass, dull spent bracken, fields bleached with the cold and seamed with another whiteness, the whiteness of snow, show no signs of life as yet. The moor is desolate under gathering fog as I go home over the top. Every day now, though, is a step towards spring, and the valley of the snowdrops a vision of hope.

✳

The solitary horseman rides up from the ford. The great cleeve towers above him in the morning light, sky and cloud rise overhead, and he moves on through the rushes, seeming to glide, too far off for any sound of hooves to reach me.

He sits straight in his saddle and man and beast are one, the centaur of ancient fable. He is part of the moor, as much one of its creatures as the red deer and the fox amongst the bracken and the buzzard in the firmament. For this is the land of the horseman. Through all time he is hunter, herdsman, shepherd, messenger and traveller, the iron-shod hooves have trampled-out our history.

The lone rider is gone now beyond my vision, and there is only the river and the brooding hills.

✳

Two red beasts cavorting amongst the redder bracken. They bound, they twist, they chase in circles, they engage in confrontation, they run hither and thither about the small combe. For one moment I think them foxes, then as they cross the stream below in flying leaps and come up towards me, I see they are not, but are two Mad March Hares.

Beautiful in the morning sun, their new and early coats red-gold, their throats and bellies white, their long ears black-tipped, they are as harbingers of spring.

✳

Having fed the bullocks on the edge of the marsh, I walk back along the hundred yards or so of river bank to the little bridge, to see that the gate that leads across it is properly shut. As I come to the bridge, there, upon the middle of its flat surface, I see a shining silver object.

My first reaction is that it is something dropped from an aircraft! Then as I step towards it I see it is a fish. A fine salmon minus its head. It has only just been taken from the river: the water still sparkles on it, the blood-juice oozes fresh from the rich pink flesh. Something has just caught it and laid it here, begun its feast, and then hearing my approach, has abandoned breakfast.

Have I an otter here? I think so. It is not the nature of a mink to bring its catch up into the open thus - it drags its prey down into darkness amongst roots - now would a fox, supposing it could snatch a fish near the bank, lay it on the top of any structure, rather it would carry it into the bushes. But it is a trait of the otter to like a table to eat upon, in natural habitat a smooth rock, here perhaps a small flat bridge.

Otters, once frequent on our rivers, are now sadly rare, though no-one is quite sure of the cause. I have not seen one directly for many years. Perhaps if I had time to study the river-banks, I might find some signs now, but oh dear, I always have so much else to do, so must leave this pursuit to others.

And the fish? Well, what would you have done? It made me three magnificent suppers.

Fire in the night. The sky above the moor is furnace-red, flames leap like hungry tongues from the hilltop and the smell of burning comes across the valley. The swaling-fires of March are eating into the heather, licking up the rush, swallowing the fern and the gorse-bushes, consuming the dry and woody growth with voracious appetite.

Though the fires have been lit with a purpose - that of burning-off the old spent growth of the years - there is something fearful about the sight and scent of fire advancing through the night with a strong dry wind behind it. A friend and saviour of life in the cold of winter, fire is a terrible enemy. Cleanser of many ills, out of control it is a ruthless destroyer. Think well before you light a fire indoors or out!

I stand for a while by the corner of the shippen looking out at the burning moor. Once in ages past such fires may have been lit by hunter-folk to drive-out game. In times of tribal war perhaps to turn an enemy advance. Again both friend and foe, the terrible remorseless power. But these are passing thoughts. My concern now is an immediate one: I have a barn one-third full of winter hay behind me. The fire is a quarter-mile off, and will stop when it reaches green pasture, but sparks fly in an east wind.

Not until the flames slacken for lack of combustible fuel and the fiery sparks no longer sail on the wind like fireflies, will I turn and go indoors. Hopefully this will be soon. Then by tomorrow's light the moor will appear black and desolate, charred to the ground. Soon though, fresh shoots will start from the roots below the soil, the moor be clothed again, and another cycle of ten or more years of growth begun.

✳

6

Catkins, softly yellow pendant on the hazel. Suddenly I see them, where last I looked I saw only bare branches. I stand under the bush gazing up at them, pretty tassels against a pale blue sky, and reach up to take a few twigs for my home vase. The first flowering of spring, they proclaim life is returning to the land.

Hopefully there will be nuts in the autumn, but that's a long time ahead, with another summer to come and go, and in the world of Nature one does not look too far ahead, but live the days as they come, one by one.

❋

Horsemen on the skyline. Suddenly they are there, though I did not see them come, riding along the rim of the world, the sky beneath the horses' bellies, the immensity of space above them. Far off, yet they dominate the landscape as horsemen always do. I feel a sense of excitement stir within me, though I know not why.

They check their movement, halt, riders sitting motionless in their saddles, then move again, and disappear as suddenly as they came. There is an emptiness for a moment, then far down the wind I hear the cry of the hounds, distant like mewing gulls, as though hunting some beast in a fabled land.

Time seems not to exist, then I turn perforce to mundane things and go on with my work.

❋

The great white clouds tower upwards from the rim of the world into a sky of unbelievable blueness, driven by the wild west wind from the sea. How shall I describe them? They are sailing galleons, they are castles, they are mountain-heads in a realm of space. They are shaded and moulded with silver and blue, and the blue of the sky above is electric, blue as though blue light were in it.

The winter-bleached rush is turned to gold where the sunshine touches it, and the small stretches of emerald grass reach amongst its clumps and tussocks, and the grazing sheep are washed white by squalls and the wind. The scent of the sea and the bogs, of wet peat and moss and burnt ground, comes down from the hill. Somewhere a bird is singing. Spring has come to the land.

Spring comes to the moor in April, or so one hopes. Even so, it is often delayed, for April, can be a winter month, here on the hills, and even May, which month the ancients saw as the beginning of summer, can still have the aspect of winter. When in the lower vales the leaves and blossoms are breaking, our upland trees are bare and the pastures bitten by frost, and the clouds can still be dark and heavy with the threat of snow.

Yet sometimes Nature is kinder, and sends us an earlier spring. Then one walks in a wakening world, and the light of April says 'Over the hills and far away ...' and the distances beckon, full of adventure, and winter is forgotten in the promise of summer.

❋

The glossy blackcock picks his way amongst the heather for what he can find. Splendid in his spring plumage, blue-black, his head crested with scarlet, his tail-feathers shaped like a lyre, underset with a fan of white, and white bars in his dusky wings, he is arrayed to attract the grey hens of his kind. Startled, he calls 'Kok, Kok, Kok' and rises with a rush.

He is our own native game bird, the blackcock, the heathpoult, at home on the moor. Soon it will be *leking* time, when the cocks gather at a chosen place and dance before the hens for their favours. Such a fine sight to see if you are lucky enough.

Alas, this is a memory from many years ago, I have not seen black game this past twenty years or more. What has happened to them all? I don't really know, but certainly the grim winter of '63 took cruel toll of them. Yet they had, as a species, survived the equally severe winter of '47. Possibly the recent diminution of the heather moor by enclosure and ploughing, also the over-burning and over-grazing of much of the remainder, has had more effect. Also the increase in predatory creatures, from magpies to mink, is no doubt equally to blame.

Some day perhaps, with care, our splendid black grouse may be persuaded to return, and I live in hope that it may be so.

✳

A mild grey day towards the spring. A soft damp fog half conceals, half reveals, the hills, and nearer to hand the land is a study in muted colours. Rush-brown, subtle grass-greens, smoke-grey depths, and trees like charcoal sketches. All is still, without wind.

As I come down the old rough track that leads into the valley and to the little bridge across the river I hear the frogs. They have awoken to their cycle of life. The whole marsh, a quarter-mile length, is alive, is vibrating with their voices. A mighty concerted purring like murmuring laughter, from all the dark pools amongst the rushes, as though the marsh itself had roused from winter sleep.

I look into the black depths between the spires, but can make out only an occasional shimmer of moving water. The frogs are ventriloquists, you never see them. So I just listen for a little while to this evocation of coming spring, then go home.

Silver withy buds against a bright blue sky. The dry black branches above the old gnarled trunks have put forth jewels upon their twigs to shine above my head as I look upwards to the firmament.

How lovely are the simplest things of Nature. No hand could fashion anything so wonderful and beautiful as the first buds of spring. The old withy that has seemed so dead all through the winter, its lower branches sprawling with the weariness of age over the rough grass and fern, touched by the sun has decked itself with pearls of silver as it did in youth. Respectfully, I reach up and ask it if it will let me have a few sprigs of itself for my vase, then carry a small bunch home to gladden the window-sill.

✳

The wild wind blows from the west, and the gulls fly inland crying with the voice of the sea. Wheeling and paper-white above the dark moor, they proclaim the nearness of the ocean.

Big herring-gulls, wide of wing and voracious of appetite, they come for what they can get: grubs on the ploughland, bugs in the rough pasture, crumbs and crusts on picnic-sites. Carrion and offal at lambing time too. (Some farmers say they will attack sheep as crows do, but I have never myself known them do this). Their tastes being similar to those of rooks and jackdaws, often they will intermingle with these and then make a pattern of sharp black-and-white over the land.

Their wild cry stirs me, reminding me of cliffs and the sea beating on the shore, and the endless rhythm of the waves, even here on the high moor. The very smell of the sea is in the wind that brings them.

As the poet saith of the sea-wind 'Come thou wind of God and strong within us stir the Viking blood' (Kingsley).

Aloft in the sky a buzzard soars and wheels, a heraldic form above the moor. His wide outstretched wings moving only very occasionally to maintain height, he planes effortlessly upon the air currents, a presiding presence on high. His form eagle-like, his pinions spread like fingers, his full span not far short of four feet, he is the largest of our hawks, and the most familiar.

Nearer to earth, there's a mewing and a piping in the top of the old ash tree. The buzzards have an untidy nest amongst its branches, and the young ones, like children everywhere, are vociferous in their demand for food and constant attention.

Now the soaring parent descends, coming to help his mate with family chores, and scans the ground for tit-bits like beetles and grubs ... or perhaps a baby rabbit would not come amiss ...

The normal buzzard colour is a buff-brown, but I once saw a white buzzard, white like a gull except for the feather tips being slightly dark. Albinism, though rare, can occur in any species, as can its opposite, melanism, for such a creature as a black fox has been known.

＊

An adder on the bank. The sibilant warning hiss as I bend down to examine some item of vegetation calls my attention to him. I back away, and then look at him. I say 'him' for I think it is a male, being long and slim. He is handsome of his kind. A bold black zig-zag all down the back of his sand-coloured body, and a V-shape on his head which gives him his alternative name of viper. Jet eyes in a small head watch me, but he makes no immediate attempt to move. He just lies still in loose coils, warming himself in the April sunshine. I guess he is newly out of hibernation, and needs the heat of the sun to give him energy. So I pass on and leave him in peace.

The adder population on and around the moor seems to vary quite considerably according to both place and time. Living on one side of the country, I never saw an adder in years; now, residing in another part, I see them often, and in spring am wary of touching leaves and grasses in rough places. Yearly too in places where they are frequent, one may see only one or two in one year, four or five together in a particular spot in another. No doubt the variations of the weather play a part.

＊

Kark, Kark! The solitary crow sits in the high bare branches of the beech tree, a sleek black bird, well-fed on the carrion of the moor. He takes little notice of me as I pass carrying only a stick. He well knows the difference between a stick and a gun.

Of all the birds of the moor, the crow is the most hated by the hill-farmers. He is known as the mutilator and killer of sheep, for let any sheep be in difficulties, rolled over on its back and wedged by its heavy fleece, or caught up in wire or brambles and weakened by its struggles, then the crow sees, and comes. He first pecks the eyes out, then the tongue, and then joined by others of his kind, rips open the belly and draws out the entrails. At what stage in these proceedings the wretched sheep actually dies no-one knows, but I have had to shoot sheep that were still alive when found thus.

Like all the corvids, crows are very cunning. It is said that if a crow is not shot in the first year of his life, then you will never shoot him and he may live as long as a man.

I once had a feud with a villainous pair that sat around watching the ewes in the upper field, waiting for an accident to happen: I'd see them in the tree by the gate as I passed carrying stick and a bag of 'cake' for the sheep. So I would go home and return with the gun instead of the stick, holding a cake-bag over my shoulder to look innocent, and come up to the gateway again. No crows. Then, a few moments later, I'd hear a derisory 'Kark, kark' from a quarter-mile away on the moor. I knew their trick, but was powerless to circumvent them on my own. They would see me with the gun a second before I saw them, and plummet straight down, then plane along out of sight on the far side of the hedge-bank, until out of range, then reappear with insolent confidence.

I never did get those crows. For a while they hung around hopefully, but since no sheep got into trouble here, they eventually went elsewhere, no doubt to plague some other farmer.

Badger Country

A spring evening with dusk coming on. Hurrying to get home before the light fades, I turn sharply into a gateway - just as someone else does from the other side. I don't know who is most surprised, I or the badger. We confront each other for a second or two, and he stares at me, his face striped black-and-white like a painted mask above a grizzled-grey body. The Brock decides it's time to go. He doubles back and goes off at a canter and I hear the drumming of his feet like the hoof-falls of a galloping horse. He is a big heavy beast, probably an old boar.

Badgers are supposed to be rare animals in this day and age, but they are not in these parts. I know of a number of setts hereabouts, all of which appear to be tenanted, and no doubt I would see quite a lot if I had the inclination to go badger-watching at night.

❋

The grey squirrel idles under a beech-hedge, fossicking for whatever he may find. His tail, the most showy part of him, is curved-up behind him in accepted squirrel fashion, a plume of black, white and silver, but his head is blunt and rat-like and not at all pretty.

For the moment he takes no notice of me, intent on what he is doing, and confident in the nearness of the low, handy beech-branches. Superficially, he is good-looking, especially in his hinder-parts, but my heart does not warm to him. He and his kind are a pest, an introduced, alien species got out of hand.

'Tree-rats' the forester calls the grey squirrels, for they are a bane to all who grow trees, damaging and destroying young saplings by both barking the branches and biting-off the buds. Worse, they raid the nests and take the eggs and kill the young of many song-birds. In proximity to a homestead, they will decimate a garden, eat hens' eggs and gnaw their way into corn-bins. So I make no apologies for shooting them when I can. This one, however, seems instinctively to know he is safe (as I am without the gun) and takes his time going off into the trees.

It is sad that the greys have everywhere replaced the native red squirrel, little Squirrel Nutkin, our sprite of the woods, who did little damage beyond the taking of nuts, and whose portrait enhanced many a child's picture-book. I can just remember the last one or two in our valley woods some forty-odd years ago, before they were pronounced extinct in this region. Just why they disappeared, or what part the greys may have played in their demise, no-one seems sure.

Vainly, I still hope that some day I may chance to see again a little red squirrel in the trees of the hanging woods of our valleys.

✳

Through the rushes on the far side of the river a black shape appears, moving this way and that amongst the tussocks in an idle fashion, and drawing near to the bank. My first reaction is 'a black cat: what on earth is it doing here on this wild reach and where has it come from?' Then it emerges into clear view on the edge of the river-bank exactly opposite me. It is not a cat, it is a large mink almost as big as a cat.

Unfortunately, I have not got the gun with me. It would be a certain shot across the ten yards of river, and the valley would be less one pest. Of all the alien pests to come into this country, the feral mink is the worst. Since moving into this area some years ago, mink have attacked fish, killed-off waterfowl and ground-nesting birds of all sorts, and decimated the poultry of the hill-farms. They are in all the streams and rivers now, and when I see any in daylight I do my best to eliminate them. They vary considerably in size, from small females the size of a stoat to big almost cat-like males. The one I have just seen was a big old"grandaddy" mink. The normal colour is dark brown (appearing black) with just a touch of white on the chin, but occasionally a light-coloured one will turn up for the record.

✳

Violets in the hedge-bank. A scatter of delicate colour amongst the first fresh blades of grass under the sear spent growth of the winter past. They come with the first touch of spring, often before the primroses, telling one with their pretty heads that the time of new life is here at last.

They are big and blue of their kind, and are I think of the sort called heath-violets. This country, with its abundant rainfall, suits the viola family. In the marsh at the foot of the big cleeve other violets grow: the little marsh or bog violet, whose flowers are a pale pinkish-mauve with delicate dark pencilling, and in places a rare white variety of the same.

Curiously, I have never come across the yellow mountain pansy, which grows prolifically in those parts of Wales similar to this country, and which I would have expected to flourish here too. Why the lack, I do not know. However, in the gardens about the moor cultiv-ated pansies of all sorts flourish exceedingly and are one of the joys of summer.

✳

Little ethereal white flowers amongst delicate trifoliate green leaves in nooks of the lane-bank under the beech. It is woodsorrel, a little plant of our western spring which comes with the violets and primroses, the golden saxifrage and the pink whortleberry bells.

It likes the misty rain and acid soil and does not care to move far to the east of our land. It grows in Ireland, so I am told, where conditions are similar, and it is probably the original shamrock of St Patrick. (Remember, the word 'shamrock' is not a botanical specification, only a colloquial term, and might be applied to any trifoliate-leaved plant of the clover or any other family). I like to think this is so and our shy little woodsorrel once proclaimed a great message and changed the history of a nation.

✳

Twilight begins to wrap the marsh as I come down to the little bridge that carries the road that leads to home. A soft mist starts to rise in the valley, and from it the trees that fringe the river-bank loom darkly.

Out of the dusk, out of the marsh, out of the silence and stillness, comes a sound like mad laughter, as though an inane and mocking presence awoke and stirred amongst the rushes. If I did not know what it was I would, I think, feel a chill of superstitious fear. But it is only a snipe drumming, making his presence known to others.

How so small a bird can make so extraordinary a sound, I do not know. Ornithologists say it is done by vibrating the feathers, but in an age before science one can understand how, heard at nightfall as I hear it now, it gave rise to belief in goblins and bog-spirits.

✳

The old, old sallow tree in the combe has put forth a shower of gold. The thin dark branches above the bowed and twisted trunk bear their 'pussy-willow' flower-tufts in a canopy of bright profusion in the morning sunlight. It is springtime again on the cleeve.

As I stand beneath the branches and look up through the soft golden-yellow flower to the intense blue of the March sky, I feel for the moment transported to Australia, for the sallow in bloom is the nearest thing I know to the wattle of New South Wales. Why it is called pussy-willow (as I knew it in childhood) I have never known, nor why it is also called 'palm'. Sprays of it, though, used to be taken to church on Palm Sunday - at which time it was usually out in flower - so presumably someone, somewhere, sometime, thought it a good substitute for the true palm of the Holy Land.

＊

Just where the little stream comes over a rocky ledge in twin cascades, an ancient alder arches over the water. The lone tree listens to the running water, and dreams perhaps of the long ago when a host of its kind choked the primeval marsh of the unclaimed valley. For the alder belongs to an older world and I am an upstart staring now, brash in the sun with sketch-book and pencils in my hand.

The alder in winter is a dark gaunt tree, but now with the touch of spring its branches are decked with fresh pink catkins, pendant in the breeze. Soon it will put forth its new leaves, shaped like inverted hearts, and there will be shade beneath it where the water-flies come and go and the dipper dives in the little pool. But I must stop dreaming and go back up the hill.

＊

A spring morning. Soft sunlight shining from an opal sky, light blue, mottled with hazy clouds of lilac and silvery-gold. The grass of the fields is emerald green and the ewes with their lambs are washed white with recent rain. The blackbirds sing from the tree-tops and the violets bloom in the hedge-banks. Life has returned to the land.

I am going on a pilgrimage. Each spring, just when the buds are breaking and the first flowers opening, I go forth to see my little secret primrose wood. No-one knows of it but me, no-one ever goes there save me alone. Only the badgers and foxes and nesting birds know of its little hidden path, only a wandering sheep or bullock ever treads this way.

Down the cleeve as steep as the roof of a house, matted with last year's old spent bracken, through the thorns that have stood so stark and black through the winter and now are clothed with living green, under the withies where the willow-warbler sings his summer song, green leaves too veiling the supple branches, by the marsh where the young frogs play, and here I am now in my little wood. Rowan and thorn, gorse above and withy below, shelves of rock and a clitter of stones, a tangle of brambles and arching raspberry canes, and here they are, the pretty ones, a scatter of delicate yellow under the scrub.

How primroses came to be here, I do not know, for there are no others nearer than nearly a mile away on the other side of the hill. The little piece of woodland is in fact quite a recent one, grown up since I first knew the spot some twenty-three years ago, its presence due to the fact that no-one has burnt-out the undergrowth here-abouts during this past time. Both the flowers and the wood are examples of Nature's ability to colonise and establish habitats. Incidentally, the development of this thicket shows how most of the high moor must have looked when first Man came this way and before he started to clear it by fire and hacking for the benefit of his grazing livestock.

As for the primroses, they are the delight of spring all around the moor. Not moorland plants themselves, they grace the woodlands and fill the lane banks all about the feet of the hills. Of all the flowers of England, they are surely the sweetest and most loved, next after the rose, our national flower. Coming at a time when we are weary of the long dark nights and short cold days and old spent vegetation, they bring us to the promise of life. 'The primroes are out' cries a voice proclaiming winter's end. May it ever be so.

✻

High, high, in the sky, above hill and combe, the lark sings his song of spring. I look upwards into the infinite blue, try to see him there, but cannot, for he is in the eye of the sun and I must turn my face away from the dazzling light. 'Hark, hark, the Lark at Heaven's bright gate...'.

Save for the curlew's cry which is the voice of the moorland spring, there is no song that so proclaims the return of life to the land than the song of the lark. When I hear it, I know that winter is past. It is the affirmation above warm earth and the sweet scent of moss and green growing grass.

All around now are the first flowers of summer. The little pink bells are on the whortleberry, the violets deck the sunny banks, shining golden celandines and soft yellow primroses show themselves in sheltered nooks. Daisies star the pastures and dandelions deck the wayside. Other birds are singing too, the leaves are green and beasts graze at peace. The dark days of winter and the bitter frosts are fled away, and life and hope beckon forward, even for me.

✳

Golden gorse in the morning sun. The bushes grouped on the hillside blaze with yellow-gold flower against the bright blue sky as I come up the slope to them, and the heady scent blows down to me.

They are aged bushes. They have survived the years of storm and fire and trampling and the delving of rabbits, and their stems at the root are as thick as my wrist, gnarled and twisted and brown, and their needles are spikes like steel. All the winter they have struggled, untidy and unloved, and now, with the call of spring they have put forth their blossom like a crown of glory.

Is there anything more golden than gorse-flower? It almost overwhelms me, scent and colour together, as I look down into it. Is there any flowering more lavish? Every sprig of bush is crammed with the yellow-gold blossom so that room could not be found for another bud. The fragrance of the flowers is the sweetness of sweet-peas, but with a slightly aromatic nuance to it, as befits a wild thing.

I sit down for a few moments, the colour around me like a peal of bells: the blazing gold of the gorse, the electric blue of the sky, the dazzling white of rising cloud-tops, the apple-green of young beech-leaves on a tree nearby, the deeper green of grass. For a moment I feel on the threshold of another world. But there's mundane work and other things to do so I must go and do them.

✳

The pair of harriers sail along the combe. Standing on the rim of the cleeve I am above them, and look down on them.

Keeping closely together, the male blueish-grey, the female deckled-brown, long-tailed, their wings nearly span of buzzards', but of finer form, they are splendid to behold. In the morning light they fly low to the ground, and their shadows run beneath them.

Whether they breed on the moor, or are birds of passage, I am not sure. Later in the year though, they come this way again, for I occasionally see them over-head. One autumn day there were five wheeling high in the sky, their wingspread unmistakable. Mum, dad, and the children, I thought, on their way from somewhere to somewhere. But only they knew where.

❋

The river runs full under the withies, noisy and foaming over boulders and rock-ledges, deeper and darker in swirling pools, alternately checking and hastening where it widens and narrows and sweeps round its bends.

Suddenly there's an arc like a silver rainbow, appear-ing for a second and gone again, lost in the hurrying waters. The leap of a salmon on its way up to the shingly shallows of the higher reaches. The fish are running now.

The salmon is king of the river. He comes from the ocean to claim his right, and I salute him on his way.

❋

Suddenly, suddenly, the tall beech tree in the combe is clothed with living, translucent golden-green, as though touched by the hand of God. The warmth of yesterday, this morning's sunshine, have at last brought forth the fluttering leaves from the long bronze buds on the dark bare branches.

For many springtimes now I have watched for this tree between the old gate and the little ford to open its buds to life. It is always the earliest of its kind to waken from sleep, veiling itself with delicate green whilst its brethren all around are still in their winter bareness. Why this should be so, why some beech trees are earlier or later than others, I do not know, but perhaps my tree owes something to having its feet by a little stream, also being in a position to be touched by the early morning sun, which is so dear to plants.

The breaking of the beech leaves cries summer to the hill-country. 'When the beech is out, the cattle go out', say the moor farmers. For it is assumed that the beech being the last of the trees, save only ash, to unfurl its leaves, it by this proclaims there is now grass enough, and warm enough nights, for the cattle to leave their winter quarters and dry diet and find Nature's fresh sustenance. (Unfortunately, this is not always so, for there may still be cold winds and the full flush of grass not yet come).

I go down to speak to my tree. The light through its leaves is surely the light of Paradise. I know of no other young leaves so lovely, so ethereal, so like a myriad fluttering butterflies. Amazingly though, these leaves that seem too delicate for this mortal earth will in a short while thicken to cast a dark dense shade, and by autumn will have toughened and hardened to the likeness of leather to the extent that they become difficult to break down in a compost-heap. The beech as a species is remarkable, for though it is generally thought of as a tree of the limestone and chalklands, here it grows vigorously in very acid soil, at a high altitude and in the teeth of the salt sea winds. It stands firm against the gales that sweep across the moor, and where it cannot grow upright it will spread horizontally, low to the ground. It is a strong grower and pollards well, and for this and all other good properties it has been much used as a cresting on the earthen boundary and field banks all about the moor, and so made our characteristic beech-hedges that are such a feature of our landscape. One warning though: beware of it in mixed planting. Because it is such a vigorous grower, and because by midsummer it carries such a dense canopy of leaves, it will tend to oust and ultimately to choke-out almost any other kind of tree, even the oak. Beauty is no guarantee of innocence!

✳

Two small birds fluttering about a patch of sheep-nibbled turf at the foot of an outcrop of rock. I focus the glasses on them the better to see them. Their white rumps proclaim them a pair of wheatears.

They will be newly-arrived and prospecting for a home. Possibly they will already have laid claim to a suitable cleft amongst the rocks. It is a wild spot here, there will be little disturbance, and there should be plenty of insects to hand as summer advances.

This pretty pair are the first I have seen this spring. Hopefully there will be more about soon, but wheatears are fewer now than they used to be. Once they were numerous, harbingers of spring all about the moor, the flit of their white markings to be seen, and the chat of their voices - very like that of the stonechats - to be heard, on any walk, but of late years they have seemed infrequent. Sadly, this is true of many of our moorland birds, and probably there are a variety of causes. I go on my way, hoping that success will attend at least this pair.

✳

Under the high beech hedge, all along the north-facing bank and spreading out to meet the old worn pasture-ground, the green mosses grow. And what a green! Emerald, apple, deep viridian, golden green and dark dusky green. All sorts and sizes too. Tall ones, short ones, soft ones, stiff ones, some like fern-fronds and some like mounds of velvet. Were I Tom Thumb I would walk in a jungle. Exotic vegetation would surround me, I would find spore-heads like strange blossoms. I would stumble amongst curious undergrowth, a world of unimagined wonder would reveal itself.

Lowly be beautiful are our mosses. Wherever there is dampness or shade there you will find them. They clothe the boulders by the streams, they hug the trunks of ancient trees, they mat the moorland grass, they smother the bogs of squelching peat. The acid soil, the damp climate, the pure air and high altitude suit them well.

The greatest moss of all, the stagshorn moss, used to grow not very far away, sprawling about rocky outcrops, its form that of a big green antler, but I have not seen it for several years. What has caused its demise, I do not know.

✳

The ewe and her lamb stand at the edge of the cleeve, under the beech-crowned bank, amongst the gorse and twisted thorn bushes. She has probably come over the bank from the lambing field on the other side by some secret gap known only to herself. The grass is always greener on the other side, they say, but it isn't here, so it must be just her roving nature that has brought her to rummage under the gorse bushes now adorned with shreds of her wool. Or perhaps, wiser than we, she seeks for herbs missing from the new grass of the field.

She is of our ancient breed, the native Exmoor Horn.

Her kind have probably grazed the moor since Bronze Age man moved up to the hills and raised the round barrows on our heights. She surveys me with what is probably ovine thought, wondering what I am going to do about matters. Dark eyes in a white-wool face look up at me, neat horns curve back from her head with something of the elegance of antennae, her fleece is soft and full, her legs short and sturdy beneath her. Her lamb is a picture-book infant. It is a white elf. The chubby little face with tiny incipient horn-buds above flicking ears is surely the face of Puck.

Mother stamps her foot, telling me to go away and mind my own business. Since I am unlikely to get her back in the field single-handed, and since the manoeuvre without first finding and stopping her private gap would be pointless, I decide to do so.

Shepherd of the Hills

H.L.B

26

The sun has gone down beyond the hills and the valley lies still and quiet in the afterglow. Most of the creatures of moor and field have retired to their rest. Then from the little thicket of withies by the stream there comes a delicate sound, a sound like the chirring of a grasshopper, like a fisherman's reel unwinding, clear on the evening air.

The grasshopper-warbler proclaiming his presence. On and on he goes, with his seemingly endless trill. How can such a little bird utter so curious and continuous a song without drawing breath? His voice keeps me company the last quarter-mile to home, then with advancing dusk he does at last stop and rest till the morning.

※

It is the time of May blossom. Everywhere the thorn trees, big and little, old and young, that have stood so bare and black through the long winter months, now put forth their summer flower.

Creamy-white blossom smothers every tree, every branch bows down under the weight of it. The heady sweet scent hangs heavy on the warm air, bees hum about the flower, ewes with their lambs lie in the shade of the boughs.

Just at the foot of the cleeve a group of thorns gather together and in their midst rises one tall old tree. She is an old, old tree. Battered by the years, her roots are twisted, her bark riven, her branches splintered and broken, yet in her old age she is arrayed like a bride. I go to her, touch her rough bark, and look up to see her sun-warmed flowers against the dusty-blue sky. Perhaps these are the last flowers she will ever bear. Yet today she stands in loveliness, the younger trees about her as her maids. Cuckoo and blackbird call to her. The young green bracken is at her feet. For one more year life is with her.

The little combe, hardly more than a goyle, narrow and deep-cleft, breaks down from the moor, and through it trickles a tiny stream, glinting in the morning light. Bushy heather grows thickly amongst the rocks, thatching them over, and rowan and thorn trees climb upwards to the sky. Sunshine and shadow meet each other across the rift.

Two birds fly upwards and at first I think them black-birds, then, as they come to rest in the branches of a tree and turn towards me, I see the white collars about their throats and know them to be ring-ouzels. Travellers from afar, they have come a long way and are prospecting for a nesting-site. I leave them to their domestic affairs, and go quietly away.

*

Bluebells on a hillside. They cover the cleeve in a mantle of blue, lapping about the rocky outcrops, spreading under the rowan and thorn trees, raising their heads above the litter of last year's bracken and amongst the new fresh fronds.

The morning sun shines down from a clear blue sky, and earth and sky seem each a reflection of the other. A few steps more, and I find an old anthill and there sit down amidst the sapphire tide. Each belled head, arch-necked upon its crisp new stem, wafts its peculiar sweet scent up to me, evoking memories of childhood. The deep blue of them all is enhanced by the fresh spring green of spires of unfurling fern and knots of young bramble leaves, and blades of springing grass. The scattered thorn and rowan trees add their creamy-white blossom to this vision of summer.

I think a little about them. Bluebells are generally thought of and classed as woodland plants, but hereabouts wherever they can find a hillside to their liking they will flourish in the open. They grow happily with bracken, bramble and small scrub but do not fraternise with the heather. One might ask, does their presence here denote that the station was once woodland, or that their more general occurrence in woodland imply that the latter is a remaining stronghold to which they have had to retreat? All I know is that they are here today, to delight me in the morning sun.

✳

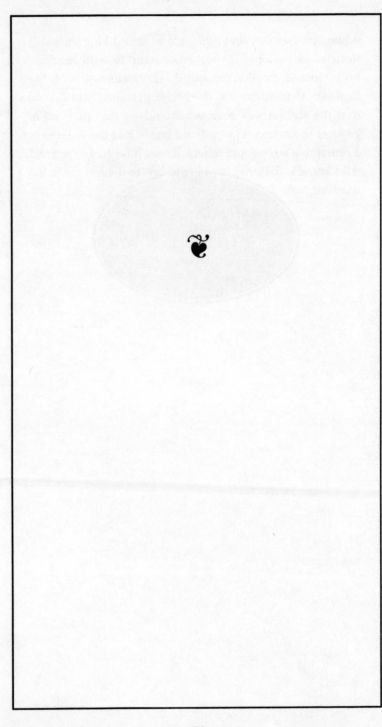

EARLY
SUMMER

Cuckoo, Cuckoo, Cuckoo! The voice of summer comes across the leafy combes of May, calling, calling, to the life of another year. Whose heart does not beat higher, whose spirit does not leap forward, when the enchanter's call is heard in our land?

Now winter is truly banished. The cuckoo brings the summer with him, so the old folk say, and takes it back again. The foolish old tale of the countrymen who tried to fence-in the cuckoo, so that summer should remain with them, comes to mind.

Tales and fancies, but the cuckoo is the bird of summer. The oldest, or one of the oldest, poems in our language is a poem of praise to the cuckoo and the spring and summer that waken to him. 'Summer is icuming in, loude sing cuckoo ...'. Through the lines of old archaic speech one sees again the buck couching amongst the leaves and fern, the bullocks gadding the pastures of fresh green, the mowing-grass blowing in the meadows, hear the ewes and lambs bleating one to another, the cow calling to her calf, and all the while 'Cuckoo, cuckoo ...'. The evocation has not changed in seven centuries.

Every year the cuckoo comes to me here, pitching in the trees round-about fairly shouting, sometimes so close that I hear the spluttering for breath at the end of each session, which is known as 'the cuckoo's curse', then see him fly off with a flirt of his long tail. Once three came together, a female who sat in a middle tree, making a curious bubbling sound, and two males who perched, one on each side of her, cuckooing against each other in competition for her favour.

Now it is sunset-time. The long rays of orange-gold reach through the near translucent green leaves, the shadows lengthen, the hills sink blue under the glowing western sky. Lambs start to nestle down against the ewes. From afar comes the evocation of a summer's evening: Cuckoo, Cuckoo ... .

33

A hot May day on the high moor. The sky is a hazy blue, the gorse flares golden amongst the rocks, the moor-grass is coming green amongst last year's old spent growth. I walk along the little sheep-path by the old boundary-wall, looking around.

In the sunshine a flight of many wings goes before me rising and falling, fluttering hither and thither. Like little birds they touch the moorland air with life. They are not birds, they are emperor moths called forth by the warmth of spring. Hopefully, I move along the wall, seeking a closer glimpse, perhaps of one that has settled for a moment on a stone or sprig of vegetation. Always though they elude me, declining to stay, though dancing all around me like will-o'-the-wisps.

After a while I sit down on a piece of tumbled walling and think of eating my lunch. One of my hands rests on the wall. Suddenly I feel a very slight touch on my thumb. I look down and, behold, there upon my hand is the emperor. So lovely a creature, wings of silvery-grey flushed with purple, upon each wing a great eye that seems almost to look at me. I sit as still as I can, whilst the beautiful visitor considers the situation. After a few moments he - or more probably she - decides to move on and takes to the air again. I eat my lunch feeling greatly honoured by such condescension from an empress.

✳

A blaze of yellow-gold at the river's edge, living colour reflecting down into the water like golden flame, rippling, glowing, reaching into the darker depths. Kingcups in May. So gloriously yellow, petals polished and shining as though with lacquer, leaves crisp and green, dragonflies for company.

I love the river-bank in early summer. Everything is

waking to new life, the water is dancing clear over its ledges of rock and into its pools and round about its boulders. Its surface is silver, its depths are amber, and one walks as though with a living presence. Every pebble of its bed shows sharp through the flowing ripples.

My river draws its being from a hundred springs high on the moor, from crystal trickles through heather and rush, from tiny hurrying streams, and now it passes me by, on its way to its ultimate bourn of the sea. I turn away from the mesmeric power of its elemental flow which would seem to draw me into it, and go home by the kingcups again.

✳

Under the bushes by the bank, just below a gap in the hedge, amongst the tangle of bracken where new green fronds are coming through the old spent fern, an antler lies half-hidden.

It is only a small one, brow, trey and upright, but a lucky find. I examine it. Its base below the burr is roughish, not smooth as when sawn from a skull, and it is not long shed. The erstwhile owner is a young stag, probably in his third year. Already loose like a child's first tooth, it would have fallen with the last jerk of the head as the beast jumped through the 'rack' or deer-gap in the hedge above.

If one had endless time to search, or was wise in the way of the deer, or was very lucky, one might at this time of year find many such antlers, from the first small spires of the young male to the splendid attire of a great stag. The cycle of growth of the antlers of the red-deer stag is one of the wonders of Nature, for the greatest 'head' is the product of just the three months' growth of early summer. As now, every antler is shed in the spring, and straight away the new horn begins to grow from the head. As the moorfolk say 'it grows with the fern', that is to say, as the fronds of the new spring bracken thrust up and begin to unfurl and stretch out, so the antler, clad in its membrane of velvet, keeps pace with it, and when the green shields spread out and harden in later summer, the antler likewise reaches its full growth and hardens, and is rubbed clean of velvet.

As to the old shed antlers, they have a mystery of their own: what happens to them all? With the annual casting of what may be perhaps a thousand stags, one would expect the region to be littered with the fallen headgear, but in fact only a fraction are ever found. Local lore has it that the hinds eat them. Possibly there is some truth in this inasmuch as wild creatures may gnaw them for calcium, and so hasten decay.

※

The eerie cry comes from the darkening combe, then the white ghost floats from the trees, across the cleeve and the stream below, and is gone again into the dusk.

The barn-owl is not generally thought of as a bird of the moor, but hereabouts one or a pair may often be seen at nightfall quartering the moorland where it laps up to the fields of the old farm. The rough pasture holds many voles and wood-mice whose kind sustain the owls, and old abandoned farm-buildings provide a roosting-place and, in a good season, a home for a small family.

The hunter of the night is silent in his ghostly flight. I hear no wing-beats, no rustle of feathers as the wide white wings pass close above me. Only the strange cry, which sometimes can rise to an unearthly shriek, calls the ear to his presence. Little wonder that long ago the bird was regarded with superstitious awe, and its appearance round-about ruins, particularly its habit of sitting in the pitching-doorway of a tallet or loft and peering-out with dark eyes in a white face, no doubt gave rise to many ancient ghost-stories.

Not long ago I had the privilege of observing a family close at hand. The local pair laid, and raised seven children, in the tallet of the old shippen here. But that's a story told elsewhere.

✳

Summer rain. At first heavy, then easing-off to a fine drizzle, settling itself to that for the day. It is not unpleasant walking in this weather, for it is mild and without wind, so I make my way down to the marsh and the river. Everything is quiet, the encircling hills are blurred with rain-mist, the world around me one of soft dripping wet, every leaf, every grass-head, every spiders' web, jewelled by the fine raindrops.

Here is the river, galloping now with the replenishment of the rain, and here reaching back from it the marsh, all heady with meadowsweet. A froth of creamy-white flower clothing the soggy ground, spreading over the rush and under the withies, intermingling with silvery-mauve water-valerian, purple horehound, yellow-gold marsh-ragwort and pink-flowered bramble. A veritable flower-garden of the wild.

How lavish is Nature in her gifts of beauty and wonder. As I return I feel that I have been given a living bounty unearned and undeserved.

✳

The young green bracken at the top of the cleeve shakes and quivers to the sound of puppy-noises.

Three little golden-coated creatures emerge from the fronds into the sunshine, pouncing, rolling and snapping. Fox-cubs at play.

Now is the age of innocence, and the world they know is only play, and the warm days and a cosy earth at night, and a mother's care, and the hard days of winter are as yet undreamed-of.

How old they are I do not know, but in sort and size they are something between puppies and kittens. The earth is not far away, but I do not see the vixen, probably she is out hunting for them, and the dog fox as well. (It is a fallacy to believe that foxes hunt only at night - hill-foxes will hunt freely in daytime when this is needful). Intent on their play they are oblivious to me, though I am only a few yards away. So pretty to watch, but time is flying, and there's work to be done, so I steal away and leave them to their own affairs.

✳

The fisherman stands, a solitary figure, upon the river bank. Silent and still, a brown-clad form, he is one with the river-world, the world of the heron and the otter, the silver fish and the wild duck, the sun on the water and the wind in the rushes.

He moves only to make another cast with his slender, graceful rod. The rest of Nature pays no heed to him, he is accepted as a part within the whole. Meadowsweet and water-valerian fill the marsh, water-hemlock decks the margins of the river, cattle graze the lower ground and sheep the higher, and birds sing from the thickets. Overhead a buzzard wheels, down to earth dragonflies hawk along the banks.

The quiet hunter is timeless within his time. His motor-car left far behind, and though his line may be made of nylon, he is again dawn-man fishing for his supper. He belongs, as do the wild things, and other men may not.

✳

Go-back! go-back! go-back! says the red grouse as he rises with others as I step through the heather. With a whirring of wings they are off and away, quickly, for despite short wings the grouse is a swift and strong flier, and has always been reckoned a challenge to the sportsman.

A bird of the north, it was probably because of this sporting potential that the red grouse was introduced to our south-western moorland in the last century. Anyway, it is good to see these red-brown birds of the heather-moor sailing away between earth and sky. They fill the gap left by the native black grouse. Yet even they are becoming scarce. Their decline is no doubt due to the same causes as beset the blackcock.

✳

The kestrel hangs in the sky like a stone suspended on a string or as a spider on its silken thread. A pin-point of life in all the space of heaven.

Though I have seen the little hovering hawk so often, I never fail to marvel and be amazed that any bird should so hold its place on high. Also marvel at the eyesight that can see, from such eminence, the small things that interest it upon the ground below.

Once I came face-to-face with a kestrel on the ground. As I came through a gateway, it was sat or perched on a tussock, only a few feet away. Such a beautiful little thing of patterned chestnut feathers, looking straight at me with big dark eyes. At first I thought it must be injured to remain so still, but as I approached nearer it spread its wings and flew away. I can only suppose it was a young one, not yet worldly-wise.

❋

The little brown mare stands in the shelter of the gorse bushes, just where the sun shines into them, making the most of the early summer warmth. At her foot is her foal, likewise enjoying the sunshine, untroubled in the innocence of youth. The gorse-bloom flares golden still and the sky is blue above. A pretty picture, but it is more than that.

She is of an ancient race. The little horses of Exmoor have grazed these hilltops since the Ice Age rolled away, before ever Man had laid his hand on the land and made his pattern of fields and farms amongst the heather and scrub. Everything about her proclaims her kinship with the wild. In height she is about 12.2hh, strongly made, in colour something between dark bay and brown, this graduating from the darkest shade near the spine to the lightest under the belly. Mane, tail and points are hard black. It is her head though, neat but deep-jawed, that carries the greatest characteristic of her kind: the mealy muzzle that looks as if dipped in a flour-pot. Her eyes too, bright and intelligent have a mealy eye-cingle about them. Her foal is reddish - he will be bay when he grows up - and his underparts all mealy like his nose, and his baby mane and brush-tail likewise black.

Though she and her kind may be nominally owned by the hill-farmers and carry a herd-brand, yet these Exmoor ponies remain in all their ways wild creatures, hardly less wild than the deer, and like the deer able to survive the moorland winter unaided by human help. But that time is not now, and the long summer days lie ahead.

❋

The sound of wings beating like a motor engine, and a guttural croaking. The ravens are flying low, just beyond the trees. Something has attracted their attention. I think it is probably the dead rabbit I noticed in the further gateway earlier this morning. If I stalk along inside the immediate hedge, I may see them closer.

Yes, as I come to a gap in the hedge I see them on the ground, two huge sable birds. Then suddenly they are aware of me, and rise with outstretched wings. They are magnificent. Black as the pit of hell, full four-foot in span, they are awesome. I see their thick-feathered throats, the hawk-like form of their wings, their wedge tails, and again hear the characteristic wing-beats, like that of no other birds. As they sail away into the sky they have the aspect and dominance of eagles.

The ravens are birds of the moor, and often I watch them. I am sure they talk, for they have a variety of calls ranging from the falsetto to the guttural. They mew, they mutter, they hoop, they bark, they croak. Also they play, twisting and turning in the air, flying wing-to-wing like stunt-aircraft, and on the ground jumping, bouncing and flapping. That they are highly intelligent, I am ready to believe. I know someone once who had one as a pet, and it was like a dog to her.

In the warm midday sunshine the bog lies dappled white as though with a summer snowfall. A myriad heads of cotton-grass look back at the sun and the sky and nod in the breeze. In freckles and drifts, from the withy-beds to the margin of the stream, about the pools and tussocks, they clothe the wet ground with their shining mantle.

I tread carefully, not wishing to take a tumble into the black squelch below, and gather a fistful of the nodding white heads for my vase at home. Then I look around. So many other little things there are to look for hereabouts at this time of year. Golden-spired bog-asphodel, bog-bean with its pink-flushed waxy   flowers, the little pink bog-pimpernel, the creeping yellow marsh-St John's-wort, the tiny blue five-leaved bell-flower, marsh-orchids, the voracious little sundew, and so many other pretty plants all among the bog-mosses. The bog is a veritable treasury of such things. Other life there is too: a tiny but perfect frog, no bigger than a thimble, hops out of my way, and there are dragonflies and insects of all sorts, and snipe rise before me.

Happily could I spend the rest of the afternoon here, but time, as someone has said, waits for no man. There's a lot to do in the garden at home at this time of the year, so I pick my way back to terra firma, clutching my bunch of white bog-cotton, and think I will have a mug of tea before I start work.

✳

The swallows fly around the barn, up to the high beam and down again, and in and out. They came the evening before last. When I counted the bantams along their roosting beam at the end of the barn, I saw in the dusk, at the end of the close-packed rank, two little white waistcoats. Next morning they were still there, side by side, and they sat there all day, a pair of very tired little

Just as the last rays of the evening sun fall on the field, across the space of the gateway, one, two, three, four, five baby rabbits come hipperty-hop in a follow-my-leader file. Seen through the shuttles of the gate they seem a living frieze. Each one is about the size of a clenched fist, with ears like two finger-tips, and a velvet-glove coat.

The age of innocence. The summer bounty, the warm nights, are theirs. They do not know that come the autumn everyone's hand will be against them. For alas, pretty bunnies grow into voracious rabbits, and rabbits are one of the pests of the hill farms. The rapidity with which they can multiply and the amount of herbage they consume, is amazing. So periodically the farmers have to have a 'blitz' on them. But that time is not now, and for the moment I can be a child again, and enjoy Nature's pretty picture.

※

Two magpies fly from the tree and wing their way across the combe to other trees, there to make more mischief, and their peculiar churring call comes back to me. It is well there are two, for this is good luck, whereas to see one is very unlucky. 'One for sorrow, two for joy'. Magpies have ever been objects of superstition.

Like Lucifer the magpie is handsome and wicked. No artist in black-and-white could have created a bird of more striking design, pied-patterned plumage and long flared tail, bold demeanour and insolent eye. I admire him greatly, love to try and draw him, but alas, he like his cousins the jay and the crow, is a predator of other birds' eggs and chicks, and probably rivals the grey squirrel in attacks on the nests of song birds. So there must not be too many magpies around, and their population need controlling somehow. But just for today I will watch the 'two for joy' and hope they will bring me luck.

swallows. Now they are up and doing, prospecting for a suitable building-site.

I think they have already decided on the place for their family home, just at the intersection of a cross-beam with the principal, for they seem to be coming-and-going from this point, and to-and-fro to the stream for mud. They twitter all the time, seemingly with enthusiasm at having found the place they were seeking.

I love to see and hear them. Good fortune will attend the household where the swallows and martins next under the eaves, so the old folk say. How many generations of humankind have awaited the swallows' return? I look up at them, think of the countless miles they have flown, the seas their tiny wings have crossed, to come again to the land of their birth, to raise their own little families in a place that is home. My eyes fill with tears, I hardly know why. The swallows have come home.

✳

The lapwings circle overhead in the windy sky, uttering their mournful cry 'Pee-wit, pee-wit, pee-wit' as I brush through the short heather and bent-grass. Others rise from the ground, disturbed and seemingly annoyed by my approach, their smart white and green-black livery sharp against the dun-coloured heath.

Then I see it, the nest on the ground, almost step on it, but stop just in time. Just a shallow scrape, holding four beautiful dark-mottled eggs. I draw back and go quietly away, taking care with my footsteps now, for there are no doubt other nests round about.

Our plover of the moor has several names, Lapwing, Peewit and Green Plover, but hereabouts it is known by another: Challacombe Horniwig. The first part of the name would seem to imply that large flocks bred in past times around Challacombe, whilst the second most aptly describes the horn-like crest on the head!

❋

The ferns at the back of the barn are higher than my head. Here, on the damp north side, with just a little sunshine at the beginning and end of the day and none in the hours of heat, they flourish and grow luxuriant. Two of the clumps are of the very beautiful delicate-fronded 'lady-fern' and the others the harder, plainer so called 'male-fern'. (Though in neither case does this have any reference to gender, and the two are distinct species anyway). Either would grace a conservatory or an enthusiast's garden, but here they are the commonplace of Nature.

This high, wet, stony, acid-soiled land is a natural home and haven for every sort of fern from the ubiquitous bracken to the tiny wall-rue. By the side of ditches rise ferns as noble as the heads of palm-trees, out of the crevices of walls and rocks and old rootstocks spring little humbler undemanding ones. Their fronds arch over streams and reach out across lanes. No hill-country garden is complete without them. Even church towers may be laced with them, both inside and out. I recall the interior of Hawkridge tower decked like a grotto with living green. Unfortunately, the ferns and the damp that pleased them were so damaging the structure that they had ultimately to be removed and the masonry repointed. At Challacombe though, the inside of the small west window is still wreathed with ferns of several sorts.

Male-fern and lady-fern, hart's tongue, and hard-fern, polypody and spleenworts of different sorts, buckless-fern, shield-fern, scented-fern and rarer ones too if one knows where to look for them, all are children of the hills. I know one last place where the maidenhair still grows, but I would not reveal it to anyone. Their uncoiling fronds are a proclamation of summer. They come with the bluebells, they keep company with the rose-red campions and white stitchworts and the tall foxgloves. All have been my companions through many years of life.

❋

The stream runs merrily over rock-ledges and into small pools, in sunshine and shade, between banks of water-plants and withy and alder bushes, and flowering elder. On a flat stone projecting into the water a young wagtail sits, neat in his new grey feathers.

Hither and thither his pied parents fly, snapping up insects and bringing them to him. They are working very hard, and need to for no doubt there are other youngsters not far off. Bringing up a family is always a struggle, whether you are human or bird.

I love to watch the pied wagtails, so smart in their black-and-white garb. Here they are in flight except for the moment of touch-down on the stone, but when they come into my garden at home they run across the spaces as though on little clockwork legs. 'Trotty Wagtail' is the name given to him or her in Devon, and in schooldays we had a playground rhyme about 'Little Trotty Wagtail ... niddle-noddle went his head and waggle went his tail ...' which describes him very well indeed!

❋

Pennywort spires rising from the coign of the old gate-way, strange little flowers from a strange little plant, but one that is a fellow-being in our western land.

In cracks in the rocks, in chinks of the walls, in stony banks, there are pennyworts, rosettes of succulent round leaves, giving rise in their time to spikes of pale green bell-flowers such as elves might play around. I look at them with affection, for they are companions of my childhood, always to hand about me. They belong to the mists and south-west wind, and are seldom to be found far from the surge of the ocean.

The size and height of the flower spikes varies considerably, I have observed, from a few inches to two or more feet, though the last is unusual. Probably soil and situation and the availability of nutrients is the deciding factor.

✳

A flit of wings, a tiny bird crossing the lane below the old fir plantation. The eye catches a touch of gold, the movement like a fluttering leaf, then the little sprite is gone: a goldcrest who has a nest and is trying to raise a family somewhere amongst the ancient battered conifers.

To have seen this rare and tiniest of birds is heartening. Once there were more of them, our little golden-crested wrens, but the alien grey squirrels have killed so many, destroying their nests and young. How I hope this little bird and his mate will survive with their brood.

✳

A group of hinds comes down to the stream to drink. They step each into the pool just where the little river curves and the bank lowers to a shelf of shingle. There are seven of them, golden as Guernseys in their summer coats, and they drink daintily, their long ears flicking at flies and to catch any sounds that are to be heard.

I look down on them from above, and because I am masked by fern and because I am down-wind of them, they do not sense me. They make a pretty picture, a summer harmony of wild Nature. Each of them, or most, will have a calf hidden away not far off, a tiny spotted thing cuddled-down in the fern where only the mother can find it. Not until it is fairly well grown does the calf run with its mother.

I only once ever saw a very young deer-calf. It was a tiny crouching Bambi-like thing, its coat of silken-velvet cream and golden-brown dappled with ivory spots, its big eyes dark and limpid, its ears like butterfly-wings.

Now something has disturbed and alerted the hinds. Heads go up on slender necks, and one, an old and experienced hind I guess, barks like a dog, a sharp staccato sound. It is a call to be on guard, and wheeling they trot away and disappear into the tangle of wood nearby.

✳

The green tide of midsummer bracken surges up from the combe, over the cleeves, and out to mingle with the moor-grass and heather above. Billowing fronds, knee-high, waist-high, head-high, stretched to their full,

Hinds crossing
a Stream

48

of a wonderful intense green, apple to emerald, vibrant in sun and shadow, toss in the breeze.

I sit down for a little while, and marvel at the fronds around me. Each is a wonder of Nature's construction. So much growth in so short a time. Such steel-like strength with delicate grace. The commonest thing that grows, yet a marvel of pattern to the artist - try to draw a single frond or a bed of fern, and it will bewilder you.

Some there are who speak against the bracken or fern (as it is called in these parts) accusing it of being poisonous, harmful to man and beast and all-invasive. As to the first, so are a lot of our lovely wild things, from fox-gloves to water-hemlock, but in my experience animals do not eat poisonous plants unless they are starving (in which case they should be elsewhere and better fed). The second is largely imaginary. The third is mainly Man's own fault. When the heather and good grass is weakened by over-grazing and too-frequent burning, then virtually the only thing that can survive and spread is the bracken. It is Man who destroys the balance.

Of course the bracken must be kept off the farmers' fields, and discouraged on the high pastures, but on the steep and often precipitous slopes it does only good, its tough root-system stabilises the soil, holding it together and preventing erosion. It also shades that soil and keeps this cool, so that when autumn comes after a dry summer and the fronds begin to wither there is a pick of fresh green grass for the hill-stock. It is cover too for wild-life, from moorland birds to red deer. Most important of all, to the wanderer on the moor, is its visual impact. Luxuriantly green now, russet in the autumn, red as the hide of a beast through the winter, it colours the seasons and at all times proclaims the wilderness. What would our hillsides be without it? For the most part a drab green or dun-colour, without character, expressionless.

So I rise and walk the little paths deep amongst the fern and wonder what mysteries lie hidden there. If some primeval life-form, some long forgotten wild beast, were to leap from the green bracken jungle, I would not be truly surprised. With these thoughts I go home.

✳

The rutted stony track curves up the flank of the hill. On one side the rough ground falls precipitously away to a stream far below, on the other the roadway is bounded by a dry-stone wall which shores up the higher ground, so preventing the soil from spilling downwards.

Here facing the sun, is a rock-garden all of Nature's making. From the crevices of the grey set stones come forth the flowers of the heathland summer. Pale mauve-blue heath-speedwell, little lilac eyebright, yellow tormentil, golden lady's fingers, white woodruff, pink lesser red rattle, slender St John's-wort and the first flowering sprigs of the royally purple bell-heather. Tiny ferns and mosses and lichens of all sorts too, all above a footing of turf like bright green velvet. Here-and-there sprays of bramble bedecked with soft pink flowers arch over the crest of the wall, giving promise of luscious fruit to come, and gorse bushes bear still their scented flower. A little higher up the hill three ash trees uphold a canopy of new and feathery leaves above their weather-beaten trunks.

So much to delight the passer-by. So much beauty for no cost at all. Why do we hanker for so many things?

✳

Six o'clock in the morning, and the sun is rising over the moor. From the distant ridges and the hidden combes comes the sound of the stirring of sheep, and of sheepdogs and of shouting men, and the wind blows fresh from the west, and carries the sound afar.

The moor has known many mornings such as this in its long centuries of being, for today is the day of the gathering, when all the hill-sheep hereabouts must come home to the shearing, and none must be left behind. Against the light horsemen are riding this way and that, distant figures in a wide and seemingly infinite landscape, whilst sheep appear and disappear and reappear again in knots and hunches, small as specks amongst the heather, seeking all the while to evade the rousing of riders and collies. Gradually the mile-wide ring of riders draws in, and nearer.

The sheep are running now, like rivulets down the combe bottoms, coalescing with others, becoming as streams, then filling the larger valley as a tide. Several land rovers now join the fray, driving out as far as they can along peaty tracks, then stopping and depositing their complement of human reinforcements in the manner of ancient war-chariots. The shouting gets wilder now, the excitement like that of a hunt, as the ovine surge comes up and onwards, held and driven by the horsemen and the panting collies. Still the wild hill-sheep would break back if they could, but they are at the holding pens now, and the gates are open. One final urging and they pour in in their hundreds.

The riders slip from the saddles, and lean over the stout-timbered corrals. The acrid smell of hot sheep fills the morning air. Once these would all have been native Exmoor Horns, but today the big flock is Scotch Blackface, naturalised for many generations on this southern moor. They are wild enough though, and horned as befits the sheep of the hills. Their amber eyes rove around the timber walls, seeking even now a weakened or unguarded place from which a sudden sally might lead to freedom.

After relaxation and talk, a move is made to complete

the second stage of the proceeding, which is that of the three-mile drive to the home farm. So now it's out onto the moorland road. Here there is a fence along one side, the near, so foot and horse together press in from the off-side. The land rovers either go on ahead or bring up the rear.

All the while, though, both dogs and their masters must be alert, for the whole flock will yet break back if it can. Not until there are hedges on both sides can the sheep be considered governable. Another hazard looms too: at one point the main road has to be crossed, indeed traversed for a way, so now there's the problem of traffic to complicate matters.

Yet on and on the procession goes, yard by yard, furlong by furlong, until at length it turns into the home lane. Then it's out of the choking dust and into the pastures above the farmhouse and the sheep are home again and all is well, and we go in to dinner!

＊

A patch of blue at my feet like the blue of gentians. I stoop down to look at the plant amongst the matted grass, and the little flowers look up at me like eyes. Germander speedwell. It is the loveliest of the speed-wells, the most intensely blue of all our wild flowers, indeed rivalling many a garden plant.

When and where it seeds in the garden, I always leave it as a present from Nature - though to be sure like all of its kindred it is a bad neighbour, choking out other plants with its mat-roots. Incidentally, I have so often noticed how very blue are those flowers, both wild and tame, which grow in these parts. Anything that has a tendency to be blue is intensely blue. (A farm not far from here has a bank of sky-blue hydrangeas by its yard gateway). Even pink things turn blue here. Someone from a distance once gave me some pink cornflowers and the next year they came up sapphire-blue! Obviously it must be something in the soil, but I don't know what, unless it's the iron.

✳

The clicketing follows me down or runs before me as I tread the grassy path between the ranks of bracken. Tic-tac, tic-tac, like pebbles clacking together. The curious sound is impossible to pinpoint, it is as though a ventriloquist lurked in the fern, throwing the noise about without point of utterance.

The voices of the stonechats are an accompaniment to the hot sunshine and scents of summer. One seldom sees them. They keep to themselves in the green cover. Only very occasionally do I see a little black-headed rufus-breasted cock perched on a gorse-sprig. Then I know his wife has a nest of moss somewhere in the thicket. But I would never search for it, for I would not disturb these little denizens of the heathland. I am content to listen to the wee tic-tac of a summer's day and know the chats are there.

✳

Forty deer in the fern. Just at the top of the wood where fire-gnarled thorn trees group, the herd idles in the morning sun.

They are mostly young stags in the velvet, but a fresh breeze blowing into the hillside prevents them being too much plagued by the flies.

Within the garland of trees where there is a little lawn-like space, some of them lie at ease, the rest potter to-and-fro picking at whatever herbage they may find amongst the bracken. Their red-gold summer coats glow in the sunshine, the cclour intensified by the vivid green all around. Their antlers thick with velvet seem too heavy for them, though not yet full grown.

It is a trying time for them, even in the pleasantness of their present surroundings, for the shedding and growing of their headgear puts great strain on their bodily economy, and if not exactly painful, is far from comfortable. Also, they need to be careful, and not damage the immature horns in any way, for this probably would cause pain, also deform the antler itself. Not until August will this annual discomfort be over, the antlers full-grown and hardened, the velvet withered and rubbed-off and the heads again have their proper dignity.

*

Midsummer's eve. The sun sinks rose-red to the hills through blue-grey summer haze and the sky above turns to a void of soft glowing gold. The world below fades now to the same soft grey whilst trees on the fore-

H.L.B.

Stags in the Fern.

ground etch black patterns in space. All is still, and quiet, save for the bleat of a lamb which has not yet settled down with its mother. Other sheep lie touched with the glow, on the darkening ground, awaiting the coming of the night.

Tonight is the night of magic. Once there would have been watchers by the stones. Once the sacred fires would have burned in mysterious places, their flames taking up the glow of sunset. A wilder world would have watched through wolf-eyes.

The sun has gone now, and the land sinks into the warm darkness. The hours of night will not be many, so if I am to arise early enough to see the morrow's sunrise, I must go home and to bed, else I will get no sleep tonight.

✳

Midsummer morning. It is but a few hours since yesterday's sunset, and the short night is fled away. The hills lie a soft grey under an empty sky, ridge beyond ridge, their streams and rivers shining silver through the white mist that fills the valleys.

I wait, dark trees and the bracken at my feet becoming discernable as a glow begins to suffuse the sky to the north-east. Now a wisp of summer cloud on the skyline glows rose-red, a moment of intensity, of waiting, and lo – the crimson ball of the sun arises over the rim of the moor: hail to the lord of the day!

Life stirs now, hill-sheep arise, ewes and lambs call to each other and prepare to move to fresh pasture. Somewhere a blackbird sings - though it is late in season for song-birds - and crows, magpies and jays begin to call and other smaller birds too. Deer begin to move towards a patch of woodland against the coming heat of the day. Far off a farmyard dog barks and cattle bawl. The first insects begin their busy day.

The sun mounts higher, highest of all this morning, for

today his days are accomplished. Soon all things will seek the shade, for it will be very hot by midday. By the same, I must go back to my breakfast, and then do whatever strenuous work is required, so that I can spend the afternoon pleasantly, down by the river, with pencil and sketchbook.

✳

The redstarts have a nest in a crack in the wall of the old barn. Every now and then I see a tail going in or a head coming out. The crevice between the stones is a very small one, hardly wide enough for even a small bird to enter, but obviously the aperture must widen out inside, giving space enough for a small cosy family home.

Now for a moment the little cock firetail sits on the bush outside. He is very smart, with his black-and-white head, rufus breast below grey back, and tail like an orange-red flame. A snatch of song, then he is off to help his wife. I hope that all will go well for them.

✳

A rose-pink wraith hovering over the twilight flowers like a tiny humming-bird from a tropic land. It is a moth. For a little while I watch this beautiful ethereal creature, until it moves down the combe, and I turn to go indoors.

I think it is an elephant-hawkmoth - surely the most inappropriate name ever bestowed on such a living thing - one of the several sorts who haunt the moorland. It is the caterpillar, though, that earns it this title, for the latter is dull grey like an elephant's trunk, quite the ugliest I know. Surely there is some moral here? Our forefathers would have thought so had they been more observant of Nature. The ugliest of creatures metamorphosed into the most beautiful. Surely the butterfly or the moth should be an emblem of our Faith. So thinking I retire for the night.

Along the banks of the river the water-hemlock billows in its heady masses of silvery-white, its flowering a proclamation of high summer. Rooted in the margins and in every wet embankments, its outliers finding a place amongst the rocks and stones of the streambed, it cloaks the river with tropic luxuriance.

I slip over the bank to stand on a strand of shingle the better to try and sketch a particularly fine clump. It rises from the water taller than I am, its heads above my head, white face against the sky. A little further up the stream some plants of musk or mimulus add a splash of golden-yellow to the flowery profusion, and a dipper flits above and then below the water.

It is almost impossible to match the profusion of flowery heads with pencil or brush, but still I try. Once someone said to me 'You never really see a thing until you try to draw it.' How true this is. Until your eyes and mind seek out the rhythms, the intricacies of any natural thing upon this earth, until your hand attempts to trace a likeness, you do not truly perceive the wonder of Creation. In the end, perhaps it is the artist who comes closest to the heart of Nature.

Water-Hemlock

H. L. B.

Morning at the top of the wood. The dark boughs of ancient oak and ash sweep down under their load of leaf to meet the hazel bush and bracken. The sound of the river far below carries up the small hidden combe, a jay calls, but all else is a green stillness.

Then, from the unseen combe, my ears catch a sound of movement. Again, and coming nearer. Something, seeming large and heavy, has been disturbed from below, and is coming upwards. I try to see through the heavy foliage, but is is too thick, impenetrable to the eye. So I wait, as motionless as I can, hoping the creature will show itself.

Suddenly, a few yards in front of me, the branches shake and push aside. The great head of a great stag comes into clear view. Monstrous in the velvet, it is the biggest head I ever saw on the hoof. Brow, bey and trey, all of great length, four and five atop, spiring upwards. For a moment he looks my way, then becoming aware of me, shears-off into the wood again.

For a fraction of time, time does not exist. I have stood in a primeval world of beasts and forests, where Nature prevails, all powerful. The noise of a distant tractor seems an intrusion from the future.

H. L. B.

In the Velvet —

The Great Stag of Druncombe.

58

HIGH
SUMMER

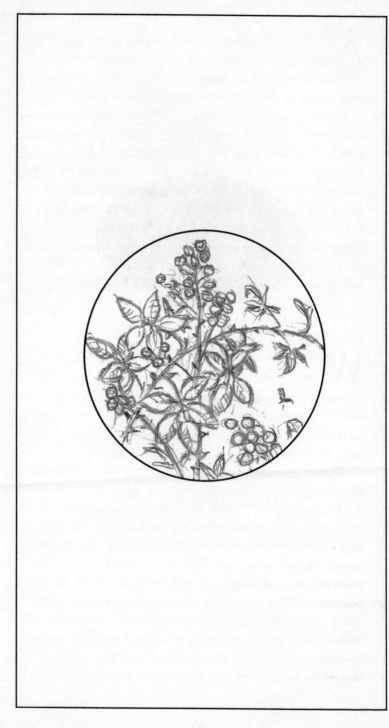

A hot summer day after a succession of such days. The haze of heat presses down on the land, the warmth of the earth comes up to meet it. A few small soft clouds coalesce out of the haze and float lazily in the light blue sky.

On the rough hillside shining grasses and small flowers mingle with a little heather and fern, and over the sward a host of blue butterflies flutter and shimmer in the strong sunshine. So lovely they are, like fragments of sky descended to earth. I watch them entranced as they fly about my feet and amongst the flowers, transported back to childhood when such a flight of butterflies was more frequently to be seen than is so nowadays. I am not sure of what species they are, but they are ethereal in their beauty and a sight I shall remember for a long time.

❋

With a flurry of wings and an indignant 'Kok-kok-kok' the old cock pheasant bursts from the tangle of bracken and rush and goes sailing away across the combe. I have disturbed him from his midday siesta, and he is telling the world about it. He probably has a wife or two not far off.

Though generally not thought of as moorland birds, wild pheasants are to be found all around the rim of the moor. In the beginning they were probably escapees from the numerous shoots in the region, finding life pleasanter away from human-kind, and the land to their liking. The country does in fact suit them, with its sheltered combes, patches of river-marsh, and tangles of undergrowth. They would possibly establish themselves more firmly were it not for the foxes and mink. Generally speaking, the cocks survive because they roost high in the vicinity of trees, but come breeding-time the hens must nest and raise their little families on the ground and then they are easy prey for vermin.

Cock pheasants can become very bold, though their wives remain shy, and at this time of writing I have a beautiful wild cock who comes every morning to my door and eats out of my hand. He first came during heavy snow two years ago, and has stayed around ever since and fraternises with the bantams – but that's another story.

*

A flash of blue across the river, glimpsed for just a moment in flight from bank to bank: a kingfisher. Perhaps if I had time to sit and wait I might see him again, this sprite of the stream, but time is pressing and I must hurry on and turn away from the water.

To have seen the beautiful little bird for just a few seconds and to know that he-or-she is there, has to be enough. The river life is less than it used to be, except on the more remote reaches, partly I think because there is more disturbance (from walkers, and from increased grazing pressure and attempted draining of marsh ground) and because of the presence of mink. I can only hope that my little bird will find a mate and be able to raise a family this summer.

*

The heat of high summer beats down on the moor. The little paths amongst the heather are bleached almost white and the heat reflects back again upwards from the hot earth. Called by the sunshine, the royal purple of the first bell-heather shows itself amongst the greener bushes of the later ling and the deeper emerald of the fern.

From the high rim of the moor the land below lies in a patchwork of summer colour, the apple-green of pasture, the yellow-gold of fields cleared of hay or silage, the richer gold of ripening corn all intermingled in small square meadows and encompassed by woods and hedges of indigo blue. The sky, bright blue overhead, draws down to meet the horizon in a haze of mauve.

The road on which I walk bends down now off the moor and into the maze of Devonshire lanes below. The sun and the heat is held between high banks, full of ferns and foxgloves, heady with tall grasses.

Foxgloves in spires and clumps, foxgloves in massed ranks like the ranks of an army, foxgloves like an advancing tide of rose-purple - how shall I liken them? They are the glory of our lanes.

I look up at them as I pass, for they are higher than my head. Now-and-again you may find amongst all this Tyrian multitude one or two that choose another colour. Occasionally I have found spires of pretty shell-pink, and once, loveliest of all, one of pure white like a fairy amongst all the rest. I look at them with respect also, for as *digitalis* their kind provides a medicinal drug used in the treatment of certain heart-conditions. Thus they combine beauty with use.

Sometimes though they need protection. Once the horrible Council sent its gnashing machines through the lanes in June, slaughtering everything, but the ensuing protest was so great that this was never done again.

✳

Ink-black clouds, heavy as night, massing and merging and darkening the already darkening twilight. The atmosphere is hot, close and oppressive. I can hardly see to finish the chores, but struggle to do so before the approaching storm, which I know is coming, bursts over the hills. I have almost done now, there is only one thing left to do, which is to get in a little bantam hen with her chicks who is reluctant to come home tonight.

Suddenly a blinding flash of blue light rends the heavens, and simultaneously a deafening crash seems to rock the world around me. I feel a tingling all through my being. That was close! I draw back into the barn. Another flash-and-crash, and another, and another. The storm has broken right overhead.

The little hen and her family! I *must* get them in. I slide round the door-jamb - it is dangerous to stand in an open doorway - and then drop to my hands and knees and crawl: I dare not stand upright in case the lightning picks on me. I flick on the torch, frail light, as I reach the end of the garden. There she is under the rose-bushes, her little ones tucked under her, too terrified to go into her coop. Now a torrent of rain descends, bursting out of the heavens, and I am soaked in as much time as it takes to tell. Mercifully she is not far from the coop. I reach out, take the chickies one by one and put them in, counting them. Now I have to get the last one and her at the same time, before either of them panics. Careful, careful. It is done. I take a deep breath, struggle to my feet with the small coop in my arms, and trot across to the barn as quickly as I am able. Home, safe-and-dry. For them any-way - now I must make a dash for my own home. The storm is moving slightly, there is a second-or-so interval between flashes and crashes now. I wait for the next flash, then run quickly across the yard. Home at last, but any-thing but dry! However, the singing kettle cheers me as I struggle thankfully out of soaking clothes into dry ones. The wind is rising now. All the elements seem loosed on the land - on such a night might the Valkyries ride.

Such storms are not uncommon on the moor. The iron in the hills draws the lightning, and the vicious force often kills livestock. In one such storm not so long ago, sixty sheep were electrocuted whilst they stood against a new wire fence: the lightning struck one end and ran along the length of it. I expect there will be tales of woe by the morning. But for the present I am home, and dry now too!

※

The big silver-washed fritillary sits on a bramble-spray amongst the bushes on a heathy bank. How beautiful she is, wings outstretched to the sunshine, a princess amongst butterflies. Golden chestnut, patterned and masked with black as though with the point of an artist's brush, she is the finest and largest of her kind to grace our summer days.

I watch her for a little while, then she flexes her wings, showing the silvery undersides, and takes to the air. Farewell pretty creature, I will look for you again another day.

※

A flick of movement at the foot of the old wall, just where the sun touches the stony ground. My eye is drawn to the spot. There in the sunshine, just for a moment, is a lizard, the first I have seen for a long time.

He is so very neat, brownish-gold, hardly bigger than a lady's brooch. Feet like tiny hands, a slim tail, tiny dark eyes that look at a huge summer world and at me. Then in a flash he is gone, disappeared into a crevice between the stones.

Once there were lizards frequently to be seen, darting across the country roads or sunning themselves in odd places, but they are scarce now. So I am pleased to have seen the little fellow today.

※

A cross the space of the open gateway, in the low light of the end of the day, a flight of small wings, perhaps a dozen pairs of them, passes from hedge to hedge. For a moment my reaction is that they are moths, then, as I approach I see that one has pitched on the top bar of the gate. It is a tiny wren.

So small a thing to live and survive in a big harsh world! Yet Jenny Wren is a dweller in our combes, and often I hear the trilling song from the bushes about the garden and glimpse the little chestnut-brown body with the tiny tip-up tail. How can such a small scrap of life survive the winters here? Alas, many do not, and mortality is great in severe weather. But those who do manage to live to the spring raise large families - like the flight I have just seen - to balance this.

Also they do have a strategy for survival: a domed nest or hollow in a bank into which they can cuddle for warmth. Once they took over an old swallow's nest in the barn. This nest was on a high beam under the roof, and was as the swallows had left it, until one day I noticed it growing a rim-wall of green moss around it. In a week or so the moss addition had become a complete dome. Initially, I could not think what was happening up there, then one day as I was peering upwards, one, two, three, four, five tiny wrens flew out of a little hole in the side!

✳

J ust where a little stream runs from the cleeve across a patch of mead to meet the river there stands an ancient elder tree. Many years have gone to its growing. Its roots dig deep into the ridge of bank by the stream, the bark of its sturdy trunk is dark and deeply fissured, its boughs bear a spreading leafy canopy beneath which cattle stand to brush away the flies.

Now, in the midsummer sunshine, it holds high a crown of creamy blossom. Is there anything more evocative of summer than elder-flower? It comes with the wild roses and the honeysuckle and the time of foxgloves and the long light days. The whorls of frothy blossom are as exotic as any blooms from a tropic forest, unpraised only because they are the commonplace of our countryside. I though, rejoice always to see the heady flower that ushers in high summer and proclaims the hot noons and warm nights heavy with the scent of hay.

Curiously, there seems to be a general dislike of elder amongst country folk. Why, I do not know, except that the musky smell of the crushed leaves may be unpleasant to some people. Certainly, there are a number of superstitions attached to the elder. It is thought an unlucky tree, for Judas is said to have hanged himself from an elder branch. Some say it is a witch in disguise, and must always be spoken to, respectfully, before cutting-down or trimming in any way. On the credit side, it is said that where an elder tree grows against a house, that house will never be struck by lightning. For practical purposes it was deemed a fly deterrent, and leafy sprigs used to be put in the brow-bands of working horses. Also, to the same end, deer are said to thrash their heads in its branches on a hot day. Another use, I have found, is to dry and strip twigs and cut them into short lengths sharpened like pencils: these can then be used as handy garden-pegs and markers, for elder-wood is white and hard, and skewer-sharp. Then, come the autumn, the elder offers a fine crop of glossy black berries for the birds, and for the making of jam and wine. So good tree, I salute you today.

✳

Along the turfy ground at the foot of the old stony bank the big beetle potters. He is huge of his kind, majestic, clad in blue-black armour like a king in his panoply. I stoop down to watch him.

He decides to assay the bank, to see if there is anything above worthy of his interest. Slowly he fumbles his way on royal blue legs, gradually lifting his black back along with them. This way and that he tries, amongst the blue-eyed sheepsbit and yellow tormentils and tiny moss-plants. Alas, it does not pay to be too venturesome: on a precarious projection he overbalances and falls to the ground upside down.

For a moment he lies there kicking helplessly, brilliant metallic blue underparts upwards to the light, then with a twig I turn him right-side-up, and leave him to go on his own way again whilst I go on mine.

✳

Green twilight. The last of the golden sunset-glow has faded beyond the coal-black line of the hills, and now the whole arc of the western sky is suffused with a luminous green. Translucent jade rising into a deeper sea-green, unearthly above the land, its mystical colour accompanies me for a while as I walk the moorland road to home. Then gradually it fades, merging into the dusky blue of night, and is gone.

These green dusks, regarded as a peculiarity of Ireland, are not uncommon hereabouts. What natural causes as to their making, I do not know, but they will appear from time to time when the sky is very clear towards evening. Sometimes there are green dawns too, when it is the eastern sky that is flushed with apple-green between black hills and the night-blue heavens. In such a light one can believe in magic and the weaving of spells and old tales told long ago.

Brilliant sunshine after rain. The light from the over-head summer sun is dazzling, and so clear there seems no distance, every ridge of the moor right to the skyline, so sharp that one might almost reach out and touch it with one's fingers. From the horizon the clouds rise up on the wild west wind, great towers and sailing galleons of white and silver-grey in an electric sky whose blue is mirrored in the glimpse of the sea to the north. The air is fresh with the smell of warm wet earth and the earth is green with growing things. At my feet the short shadows are almost black, and fringing the road-bank the early bell-heather splashes the moor's edge with royal purple.

A buzzard spreads its wide wings and rises into the air as an evocation of the moor. If the red stag should be the proper heraldic device for Exmoor, them the buzzard should surely be its crest.

I feel I could walk for ever on such a morning, but time is slipping away, and there are other things that must be done.

Skylines

A sweet scent like the scent of carnations comes down the hillside to me. I look up to the little boggy patch where a rill of dripping water comes down to spill in the gutter of the old stony track. Then I see them, the spires of the yellow-gold bog-asphodel rising from the matrix of moss and sedge.

So pretty they are, wafting their sweet smell on the evening air. The small golden red-antlered flowers have something of the character of minute lilies - the plant does in fact belong, I believe, to the *Liliaceae* - and the leaves likewise complement the likeness. In their damp nook they hold place in the community of the moor, rarer though than they used to be.

Once the whole hilltop above, wet boggy ground, carried them in their thousands, and from my garden below I would smell their perfume blown on the west wind of summer. Since then, the high ground has been drained and ploughed, and the asphodels have departed with the cry of the curlew.

※

Picking worts in the sun. The sky above is very blue, the road edge at my feet dry and dusty. The bank is head-high, clothed in a mixture of heathers and whortle-berry bush, and I do not have to stoop to pick.

Whortleberry grows well on a bank. Here it has fair drainage and catches the sunshine. I work my way along the bank pleasantly, turning the small leaves with my fingers to find the blue-black fruits. No, I don't gather them into a container, I just pop each delicious little berry into my mouth as I find it. For myself, there is no point taking them home - I much prefer them raw, and I'm no hand at cooking anyway.

Once though, worts were one of the harvests of the moor. Whole families would turn-out in berry-time to

70

pick all day, breaking the tedious work with a midday picnic in the heather. Some of the fruits they would keep to make jam and pies, some they would sell in the townships to gain a little extra money wherewith to buy necessities for the winter.

I have no need for either, and the little berries, blue with the bloom of freshness, are for me a delicacy to complement in taste the visual pleasure of the purple bell-heather amongst which they grow.

✳

The scent of the bog comes fresh on the wild west wind as I come up to the high wide top of the hill: the smell of rain and sun on acid wet ground, of peat, moss and rushes, and the distant sea.

Here on the roof of the moor there is only space and the sky. I walk carefully. At first there are rushes to tread on, which I do, turning the rush with my foot for a purchase on the clump, avoiding the soggy hollows between. Now the rush itself peters-out and there is only sedge and squelching black mud and pools reflecting the light like fragments of mirror. Now peat hags and hollows, and mounds and sheets of sphagnum moss. I go even more carefully. The ground such as it is, sucks at my feet and I come to a patch which seems to float like a raft. I have come far enough, looking for rare bog-plants. It is time to pick my way back.

I take my bearings carefully, by sun and by what little I can see of other hilltops. Which is not much. The hills which comprise the high moor tend to be flattened at the top, so that though the flanks are steep to come up, the summits are mostly plateau-like, and there is little to be seen except clouds and the infinite sky. It is this which gives the sense of limitless space, of walking into the sky, which on a day of great cloudscapes induces such exhilaration.

Home again, I consider the question, how dangerous are Exmoor bogs? I don't know. I give them the benefit of the doubt. The image of Carver Doone's final fate in the black bog must ever be with the reader of Lorna Doone. There are more mundane tales of cattle being sucked-down, and one of them at least I know to be true. Certain bogs will swallow sheep. I remember well picking my way through the bog a half-mile from here, and seeing what I took to be a white stone amongst the rushes and sedge, but on looking closely saw it move. It was the head of a sheep. All the rest of it was drowned in a small pool of liquid black mud. How to get it out, poor thing? I took off my jacket and sprawled on what I hoped was firm ground, or firm enough. Reaching down I tried to get first one, and then the other, of its forefeet up and onto a clump of rush, and then, clutching at the soaking wool, heaved. At first I did not think I could manage, for the bog always sucks downwards (and I had to be careful not to go in myself), but the poor beast in its ultimate terror began to struggle wildly and with a concerted heave, out it came, and lay exhausted in the rushes. (It afterwards recovered, I'm glad to say). As it had struggled-up I fancied it was standing on something, so I felt down, arm's length. There was another sheep there quite drowned. So just this eye of bog must be some four feet deep. The whole expanse is sixty or more acres, and has a bad reputation. There are remembrances of the mounts of unwary riders being bogged up to their flanks and having to be got out with ropes.

The hazard of getting anything out is the danger of going in yourself. I recall another instance when a farmer I know drove his land rover too close to a bog and got it stuck. He walked home and fetched his tractor to heave it out - and got that stuck. A neighbour then brought his tractor to help, and got that stuck as well. A breakdown firm was then contacted, of which the first vehicle to come and reconnoitre got stuck too. In the end it took the most powerful machinery to rescue all four vehicles. So treat bogs with respect!

*

Jewel-like the red raspberries cluster under the silver-backed leaves on bending canes, all amongst the tangle of bracken at the foot of the cleeve below the rocks.

How exquisite their taste! No cultivated berry has quite such a flavour. They are food for fairies. I eat sparingly, for I feel I am cheating the birds if I take too many. Yet I might fill a big jug if I would, for they are prolific hereabouts. Indeed here, as in many other parts of the moorland country, the wild raspberry is more common than the ordinary bramble. Once country folk went out to gather them - as they did the worts - in quantities to make into jam and preserves, but I think it a shame to treat so delicate a delight thus (cultivated varieties are good enough for cooking) and prefer to savour them one by one in the sunshine of an afternoon walk.

*

Water plants fringe the stream, a margin of pebbles marks-off the rippling water from the land, and big withies group together to bound the scene. I slip down onto the strand the better to find a position to sketch the sunny reach, and to this end move around a big head-high stand of vegetation. Suddenly, as I do so, a startled heron rises from the spot, almost at my feet, where he - or she - had been fishing.

He wheels over my head enormous at such close

quarter, heraldic, plumed head drawn back, beak like a stilleto, neck curved like a swan's, wide wings arched in powerful flight, feet trailing on stork-legs, a painted creature of grey, white and black. As he beats away to another part of the water, he seems a very evocation of the river in all this lonely marsh and valley.

✳

The little withy at the foot of the combe is broken and frayed, its branches cracked, its bark hanging in shreds. It looks as if it had been attacked - which indeed it has. I can guess the culprit well enough: a stag, possibly a big one, probably now lying-up in the fern and scrub higher up the combe.

For this is one of the signs by which a stag may be located at this time of the year. When the antler is full-grown, the velvet membrane which has sheathed and nourished it withers and dries, and the beast then frays it off by rubbing on any branches and projections he can find. So this little tree has been the fraying-stock of an irritated and large stag.

✳

The full moon rises rose-red into a sky of midnight blue. A crimson orb above the coal-black rim of the moor, it is like an omen in the heavens, unearthly, a portent of some mighty happening. I rest awhile sitting on a hillock amongst the heather and contemplate this phenomenon. I have seen pink moons before, but never one so nearly blood-red as this. What mysterious element presents it thus? I can understand how the ancients might see such an appearance as presaging a momentous event.

All is quiet, but along the far boundary-bank something

moves. Deer? Probably, but I cannot see them clearly.
Time to be going, or I'll not be home this side of midnight.

✳

Butterflies. In the hot sunshine a lovely Painted Lady
sits on a spray of heather, wings outstretched, a queen
amongst her kind. All around lesser butterflies of other
sorts, brown ones, russet ones, small blue ones like chips
of sky, flutter hither and thither, seeming as courtiers
dancing attendance upon her.

Blue sky, the sweet scent of the heather, the dappled
movement of living things, how beautiful they are. Why
do we care so much for money-bought things?

✳

By a patch of rushes a small rabbit rushes hither and
thither in a sort of crazed circle, uttering squeaking
cries. It is unusual for a rabbit to 'speak' except in extrem-
is, so I go across the grass to see what ails it. Then I see
the stoat. There he is, as yet unhurried, handsome as
Satan in his coat of red-gold, chest snow-white and tail
black-tipped. His black eyes in his almost snake-like head
hold the rabbit in terrifying thrall.

Oh silly little rabbit, why don't you run away? Bunny
seems incapable of rational action, but nearing the rush-
tussocks does make one effort to hide. The stoat follows,
and I know what the end will be.

What is the extraordinary basilisk-power that a stoat
exercises over its victims so that they either stand still or
run in demented circles? Faced with any other threat,
rabbits will streak hell-for-leather out of harm's way.

✳

Bees in the heather. The busy hum, the shimmering movement, the amethyst-purple flower, the heady wine-like scent, the warmth of the sun, together under the blue of the sky, make a dimension of life all their own.

Over the boundary wall, within the enclosure of the old farmstead, amongst crumbling grey walls and the wind-battered trees, stand a hundred hives. Some firm has rented the old site for the summer and here transported all its hives. This too is a harvest of the moor.

To-and-fro fly the honey bees, ceaselessly carrying the nectar of the heather to the hives. Heather-honey is the richest and most desirable of all our English honies. Strong and deep golden-brown, its taste carries with it the tang of the moor and seems to hold within itself all the warmth of a summer's day on the hills. I skirt quietly around the enclosure, not wishing to disturb the bees, though it is said that bees will not attack anyone who is not afraid of them, and go on my way. Good busy little bees, bless you for your labours, and I hope someone will give me a jar of heather-honey for a Christmas present.

Head Lowered

Head Raised —

H. L. B

Aspects of Antlers

Dawn and deer. In the strengthening morning light a group of stags idle at the edge of the wood, prior to seeking green shade against the heat of the coming summer day. The first rays of the rising sun catches at their bright golden coats and touches their white-tipped antlers. There are five of them, two big heavy-antlered stags and three lesser ones. I reach for the glasses the better to study them.

Their antlers or 'heads' are clean of the velvet now, dark-beamed and bright-pointed. As one or other of them lowers his head, one can assess the antlers he carries. (This is the best way to assess a stag's attire, facing head-on, the head being lowered as in grazing, or when mounted trophy-wise, as one will see on the wall of many a farmhouse). For thus the number and setting of the points can be readily seen.

The biggest beast has 'rights' with two and three atop - eleven points - and the next in scale rights and two atop on both sides: a good ten-pointer. The others are youngish males, carrying only small heads of six or less points.

H . L . B .

Yearling .   Spring Stag   Pricket

77

It is when the antlers are hard, clean, and full-grown, as they are now, and will so remain through the autumn and winter, until they are shed again in the spring, that one can make a guess as to the age of the beast and follow the sequence of annual growth in general. It must be remembered though, that one cannot tell precisely the age of a stag from his antlers, for much depends on the individual and the circumstances of his life.

However, a rough guide may be as follows. In his first year he is a calf and carries no horns. In his second he is a yearling and throws short spikes. In his third he is a pricket and carries uprights and a brow. In his fourth he is a 'spring stag' (so called because such a one is hunted in March and April) and should have brow, trey and at least one fork at the top. In his fifth year he is a 'warrantable stag' and should carry 'all his rights' - brow, bey and trey - and two good points atop on each side. Thereafter he may increase the number of points atop, until overall he may carry a head of anything up to sixteen or even eighteen points (though such a number is very rare) until, with extreme old age, his head may 'go back' and become poorer.

Again, though, it must be emphasised that a stag's antlers are not an absolute guide to his age. Various factors contribute to the growth of the head: heredity, feeding, hardship or otherwise, and accident. As, for instance, a beast who has fed well under favourable conditions, will grow a better head at an earlier age than one who has had poor pickings. Damage to an antler when in the velvet can deform it in whole or part.

For me, the antlers of the stag have an almost magnetic attraction. A glimpse of antlers, held high on a beast moving in the fern, or set as a trophy upon a house or stable wall, never fails to stir some atavistic instinct deep within, and to excite me, and I never lose a chance to make a sketch, either directly or from memory.

Thick heavy Beam of the
head of a Stag who has
had good pickings

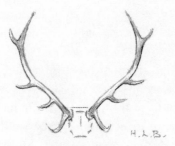

H. L. B.

The light whippy head of
a Stag who has had
sparse grazing.

A Contrast in 10-pointers

EXMOOR ANTLERS

Shving Stag —
Brow, trey fork
and upright.

A good Ten-
pointer — Brow
Bay Trey (Rights)
and Two Atop.

A Fine Twelve-
Pointer — all his
Rights and Three
Atop.

Ten-Pointer,
Uneven, Three
Atop near-side,
but lacking bay-
point

Ten Pointer,
Three Atop but
lacking Both
Bay Points

80

Twelve~Pointer, uneven, narrow, a rather ugly head

Thirteen Pointer, long Bays close to Brows, too wide unbalanced

A very fine Fourteen~pointer

Eighteen~Pointer, Tops palmated, the head of a big old Stag

The Head of a very old Stag, 'going back'

81

They are wonders of Nature, and no two heads are exactly alike. What makes a fine head? Beam should be strong and heavy, in form fine and spreading, neither narrow nor hooped, and the points long, not short and stubby. All the 'rights' (brow, bey and trey) should be present and the overall number of points even and well-balanced. Texture and colour dark and rough, with the point-tips white and polished.

A fine head should have at least three atop each side, making of it a twelve-pointer, and there may be four or five to a really great head. Number of points alone though do not make a great head. I once saw an eighteen-pointer, but it was not a particularly beautiful head, as the tops were palmated, so that the points appeared short and stubby - the head of a big old stag.

Now and again one comes across deer with odd or freak heads. The beast known as a nott-stag is one such: he is a male who never throws antlers longer than short stubby projections, and who may be mistaken for either a yearling or a hind, (though he may in fact be of mature age). Another is the one-horned stag, who may have one good antler and only a stub on the other side. However, these undesirable sorts are usually culled-out at the beginning of the hunting-season.

✳

Heather in high summer. Here I sit on the hillside and it is all around me in royal splendour. I rest on a ridge of ground and look at the scene before me: purple hills to the west, a valley below thick with oak woods, a farm enfolded in the midst, and a moorland road twisting its way from here-to-there.

As the great clouds wheel across the sky, wind-driven from he western sea, the pattern of colour shifts and changes and changes again, ever moving with the running light. Rose-bright in the sunshine under a cerulean sky, mauve-purple in the shadow of indigo cloud, the heather has many shades of colour. The west wind blows the scent of it too, sweet as honey and heady as wine, across the land.

A feeling of exhilaration takes hold of me, a lifting of the heart, a delight in the colour and scent, the warmth of the sunshine and the freshness of the wind, the space as wide as the sky. Yet it is not the delight to the senses alone that exalts. There is a deeper response stirring within. The purple heather in its glory, crowning the hills, sweeping across their flanks, patching and decking the wayside, speaks to one's inner self of freedom, lack of restraint or confinement, and proclaims a world where one may go where one wills, stepping between pleasure and danger, seeking for adventure.

I bestir myself to pick a small bunch of heather to take home. Here, almost within arm's length, intermingled with Nature's tapestry of damp golden gorse, sprigs of green fern and moorland mosses, I can find all three of our native heath species. First, right beside me, gloriously royal purple, is the bell-heather *Erica cinerea*. This is the earliest to come, sprigs of it appearing sometimes as early as midsummer, and the longest to last, flowering tufts of it to be found even in October. It likes best a dry sunny bank and flourishes, as here, in a raised position.

Next, nearby, is the common heather *Calluna vulgaris*, whose amethyst flower makes great sweeps of colour, across the August hills. Its season is shorter, coming far later and going earlier than the bell-heather, and it is more tolerant of damp, though likewise it does prefer dry land.

A little way away, in a damp patch, grows the third species, the pretty rose-pink cross-leaved heather *Erica tetralix*. This too is a bell-heather, but unlike its purple relative seems to prefer a damp position and is indicative of wet ground.

Like all things in Nature, occasional variations of colour may occur. I have found, from time to time, pure white bushes of each of the three species, also a crimson-red form of *cinerea*, and once a lavender bush of *vulgaris*. A few fronds of fern plucked and set around my fistful of heather completes the bouquet, and I rise and go home.

✳

The summer heat fills the combe. I push my way down the rough narrow path through waist-high bracken, tussocky heather, and green gorse. Here at my feet is the little stream, only a few feet wide, with a tiny level ford leading on to the rising path on the other side. The water is low, murmuring over rock-ledges, and each rim and stone is clothed in deep green moss. I kick my boots off (they leak) to stand in the water the better to look up the pretty stream. The water is crystal clear, and I drink a little of it for refreshment, and as I stand upon a stone my bare feet sink into the deep emerald moss as in a velvet cushion. To one hand a beautiful fern spreads its fronds, on the other a single splendid foxglove stands, tall as I am, drawing the eye with its rose-purple spire. A knot of rowan-trees fills in the picture.

It is a place and a moment of enchantment, and I long to linger, and with reluctance tear myself away! Time! There is never enough of it. So many things to do that must be done, but at least a memory is for ever.

✳

Purple heather high under the sky, summer clouds soaring upwards into the blue of space, a west wind from the sea whipping the fragrant scent across the land. Two objects converge and meet in the midst: a horseman and a land rover. Greetings are exchanged and the rider slips from his saddle and leans on the vehicle for a gossip with the driver.

The bay horse is dark against the light, its saddle shines

in the sun, the heavens are under its belly. Space and being are one.

Horse and vehicle, rider and driver, both belong where they are, each the expression of a land that is wide and wild, where men herd for a living and hunt for sport. After a little while, more likely a considerable while - for time has little meaning in this setting - conversation slackens and the rider mounts his horse again, the land rover roars into life, and each of the hill-farmers goes his way across the moor. There is only heather and sky and the wind.

✳

Dragonflies hawking along the river banks. Vivid beautiful predators, purposeful in their flight, flashing their colours as they move this way and that. There's the big black-and-yellow monster, the tiger of the air, his big eyes seeking for what he can devour. Then comes another fellow, just as big or bigger, superb in electric blue and golden-yellow, a marvel to behold. Then the smaller demoiselle, many of them, some flaunting iridescent blue-green bodies under black gauze wings, others fiery red like scraps of flame.

How wonderful they are, these forms of life so different from our own with whom we share the river's edge, the bright water, the shadowed brink, the tall and shining grasses, the summer flowers of the margins. It is their world, and I the intruder, so I tread softly and with respect.

✳

Across a patch of bright green grass runs a hurrying red-gold fox. Something in the combe below has disturbed him and he stands not upon the order of his going, but makes haste for the cleeve on the other side of the hill. He is a summer fox, his coat like golden orange peel, his mask and pads touched with black, his throat snow-white and a fine white tag to his brush to finish him off.

A very fine villain he is, a wary dog-fox, roused from his daytime nap somewhere under a bramble bush and no doubt resentful thereof. (I can now see walkers in the combe). He will not go far though, and will very likely come back to his favoured place before long.

One does not often see a fox in the open on a summer's day, so I am pleased to have seen him now, but hope he will keep away from my home and hens.

✳

The cry of the hounds comes over the moor. Last night the crescent in the sky proclaimed the hunter's moon begun. Now the morning's sunlight touches the flecks of gold in leaf and fern, speaking of the autumn days to come.

The deer lift their heads and prepare to move, all but the old stag. He will not move until he is forced to do so. Many years have made him wily and knowledgeable.

The younger deer are on their feet now, loping with easy stride through the high fern, the bright sunshine playing on their red-gold coats. They will not go far, only to the next patch of cover. Intuitively, they seem to know it is not they who are being sought-for. One young male deer remains, the old stag's squire, and stands uncertain. Now the big hounds are crashing through the brake, pied bodies amongst the green and russet, giving tongue at the scent of the deer. The young stag takes-off, fleeing with the swiftness of youth, and the tufters follow him. But the sharp eye of the huntsman on the rim of the hill sees, and calls them back.

Scarlet coat like a splash of blood in the landscape, the huntsman rides further down, his horse's hocks and quarters tucked in under him on the precipitous cleeve. Voice and horn encourage the hounds to try again. Once more they are in the thicket, closer, tighter, and the big stag knows it is time to go. With a sudden bound he is up and away, great antlers laid back under the oak branches, and his face set towards the open moor beyond which lie the greater coverts of the farther valley.

Huntsman and another horseman ride hard to stop the tufters as they reach the open, and the big stag goes on alone through the heather.

On the hill the pack is waiting, eager, held and steadied by the red-coated whip, alert for the summons. It comes, with a galloping horseman pounding up from below. Now hounds are on the move, white and tan in the ling, and as they come to the line where the tufters wait, they own it with a great cry and are away. A hundred horsemen move along the skyline.

What will be the way of the chase, how and where will it end? How many of those who rode to the meet will finish with the hounds and come home with them? No-one knows, no-one can tell. Only the moor, with its hills and valleys, its rocks and streams, its wild things and sudden storms, can answer this.

" All his Rights and Seven on Top "

Red as blood the rowan trees rise from the rocks where the river bends its course about the bluff. The slender branches above the shining silver trunks bow down under the weight of the massed and scarlet berries as though the burden was almost more than they could bear. Earthwards, the clutching roots twist into the crevices, struggling for a foothold strong enough to stand against the storms, then delving as deep as they can into the thin stony soil to find sufficient sustenance for life.

How courageous they are! There are no other trees that could or would root themselves in rocky outcrops, then raise stem and branch and head to battle with the stinging, battering winds of moor and sea. Well do they earn their name of mountain ash.

Through winter their bare branches fight with the storms and blizzards, in spring they put forth green leaves, in summer they bear creamy blossom, then, as August turns to September, they receive their crown. The berries they have nurtured turn to glorious scarlet, a gift from Heaven, one feels, for their courage.

I clamber up the bluff to commune with them. The sky above is blue amongst the laden branches, the earth below spattered with fallen berries as though with blood. I touch their trunks, surely the polished work of silver-smiths. They rise in their generations, ancients gnarled now from many battles with storms and browsing hill-sheep, younger trees in prime of life, and younger still, striplings of a single spire, just starting out in life. I sit in their shade for a while, amongst the tussocky heather and fern that patches the rocks, and listen to the river running below, blue as the sky and dancing over its boulders.

A moorland idyll. I feel the magic of the little trees. The rowan has always been held a fairy tree. It has been said to stand sentinel at Heaven's gate. Sometimes its kind were planted about a homestead to keep witches and warlocks at bay. You made a 'wicken cross' to hang above the house door for good luck and to keep evil away. (This was two small pieces of rowan-twig tied together by red thread). A rowan tree must never be harmed, for upon the person that did so, ill-luck would fall.

So I say good-day to them courteously, and come down again to the road.

✳

Twenty horsemen galloping through a gateway. The earth shakes as they pass, hooves drumming like thunder. Flying black mud, panting breath and flaring nostrils, the sheen of sweat, the glint of steel, the rasp of leather, the enormous strength of bone and muscle: the magnificence of animal power.

The excitement of the moment courses through me as I stand by the gatepost, only inches from the straining horses and the riders in their saddles. Far away the note of the huntsman's horn calls them on and soon they are gone beyond the skyline and there is only an empty gateway on the moor again.

✳

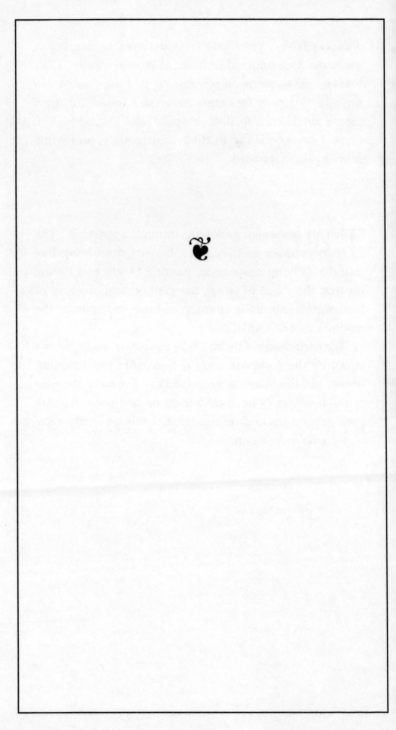

AUTUMN

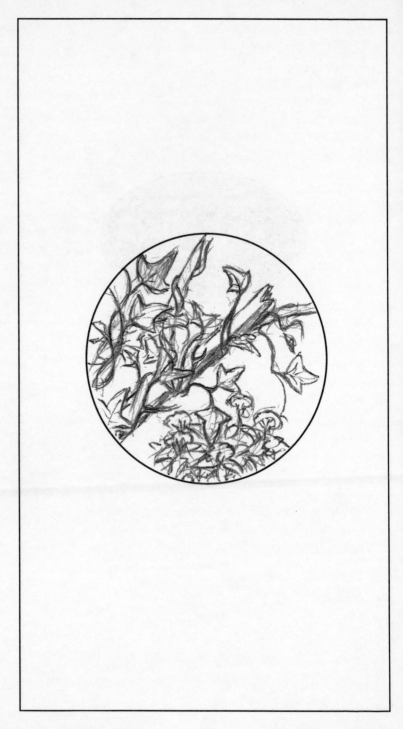

Here I sit in a favourite place on a patch of turf in a half-moon hollow amongst the rocks. The sun is hot, held as in a bowl, and heather clothes the rocks above a circling sea of green bracken from which rises a single golden frond as a herald of autumn. Below the river curves and runs with murmuring voice, and beyond it the great hollow cleeve bounds the valley with indigo shadow under a bright blue sky.

It is a place and a moment of delight, and I am bent on making a colour sketch to remind me of its pleasure in the darker days of winter. Paint-box, paper and board, small jar of water with brushes, all set around, so no more excuse not to make a start. So a start I make. But oh, how hard it is to match, to capture, the colours, the intricacies, the subtleties of Nature! The colours, the very forms, seem to change as the sun moves imperceptably on its course. Hardest of all is the bell-heather. Try as I will I cannot get a true likeness to its glorious purple. It is beyond the capacity of pigments to recreate the living colour. However, I do my best.

For variation I study the rocks. Jutting through the surface soil and vegetation they are the bones of the land. It is they that give form and uphold life and make a landscape. The old sandstone and its shale are here grey and patched with lichens, strange encrustations in patterns of black and white and yellow and gold. Lowly forms of being though they are, they are part of the living world and touch the rock with life.

The sun is drawing down to the rim of the hills. I have spent far too much time here. I rise and go.

＊

Ek-ek-ek-ek. The strident call makes me look up. The hawk flying high is a dark silhouette against the

cloudy sky. Scythe-wings, streamlined tail, swift movement and a seemingly angry voice. Now the bird
descends, flies this way and that, changing direction with
amazing rapidity, then shears-off into the further valley.

There is no mistaking the peregrine. The lord of the air
is rare but sometimes to be seen, as today, for it is a bird of
moor and mountain, and nests - or used to do so - on the
cliffs of the coast hereabouts. Once, a long time ago, I saw
a pair at Landacre Bridge, and it so happened that I was in
company with a friend who had practised falconry, and
he identified them for certain, where I might not have
been so sure for myself.

✳

Blackberries like polished jet, blackberries in pendant
masses, blackberries in festoons, blackberries galore.
Here in the sun on the warm hillside the arching brambles
tumble down from the hedge-bank into the mass of
bracken, laden with their autumn fruit.

Is there anything more delicious than a ripe sun-
warmed blackberry? I think not as I pick handfuls of
them and then eat them one by one, savouring each. I
suppose if I were a good housewife, I would pick a big
cargo of them and take home to make into pie, jam and
jelly, as the goodwives used to do, but I like my fruit raw,
so prefer to eat Nature's bounty fresh from the brambles
as I walk.

In doing so, I have observed that there are several sorts
of blackberry on and around the moor, at least three of
them sufficiently disimilar to be regarded as distinct
species: there are those such as I have just been eating,
luscious big thimble-size-and-shape, whose juice is purple
black, borne on brambles arching head-high; there are
those that are small and crimson-juiced, set on low grow-

ing brambles in a mat with other moorland growth; and there is the third sort that has the appearance of a raspberry only disclosing itself as a blackberry when it finally turns from red to black, though its juice remains bright red. All are fruits of delight!

✳

Storm. All night long the gale has torn across the land, flaying the moor, howling down the combes, roaring in the trees, ripping-off roofs and battering everything. Now a wild red dawn, and no abatement of the wind. Out of the west, it comes with the rhythm of the sea, terrifying gusts crashing like waves, then sucking back for a moment of frightening calm, to come again with almighty force. All trees bend before the wind, the last of their leaves gone, their branches flailing while their roots clutch desperately in the earth. Mostly the beech and oak hold fast, but there's a crash as a big overgrown withy is torn from its socket in the bank and goes sprawling, root upwards, on the ground. Another crash as the top half of an old ash tree splits from its trunk and rolls over and over into the combe as though with waving arms. Now a sheet of loose tin on the shippen roof is clanging wildly, adding to the cacophony of sound.

Everything that can find shelter has found it. Deer down in the woods, ponies in the goyles, sheep and cattle under the banks, foxes and rabbits underground. Where the poor little birds can be, I don't know, yet when the storm abates, tomorrow perhaps, they will appear from somewhere. Humans too will emerge to assess the damage, clear fallen timber, and repair roofs. Life is tenacious.

This land has known many storms for it is a land of storms. Hills rising to 1700 feet and an ocean coast not many miles away make it so. Whatever wind that blows batters at it. Gales, blizzards, thunder and lightning and flood, all have formed it as it is. The outcrops of rock scoured of soil, the rivers spilling from the heights, the combes cleft deep, all testify to the violence of Nature. The farmsteads with their sturdy buildings, windbreaks, roads, and high-banked fields, have all been established and maintained in a battle with hostile elements. Each is as a fortress against the power of a primeval world. Someone once said to me 'this is a country where one feels the force of Nature'. How true this is.

✳

The cattle are running now. Over the shoulder of the hill, over the rim of the brake, now they are plunging down the cleeve, crashing through the belly-high bracken and bramble and old twisted gorse. Great red bodies in deep green fern, long white horns flashing like scimitars, roaring wild-beast bellows and a heavy thundering of hooves. Altogether some thirty cows with thirty calves and a mighty bull in the midst.

It might be a scene from the primeval past, it might be looking through a gap in time, seeing again a trampling herd of the great wild cattle on an ancient land. But time is timeless, and the herd we are shifting are our own red Devons of today.

They are a native breed, old in the context of history, and belong to this land of hills and valleys. For centuries they have grazed the pastures of the hill-farms and filled the shippens on the winter nights. They have provided the country with fine beef, also milk, butter and cheese, and, in earlier times, they ploughed the fields in long toiling ox-teams.

Alas, we live today in an age concerned with quantity

at the expense of quality, and the herds of Devons grow less each year to be replaced with ugly mongrel stock. The few that are left are mostly polled or dehorned. I will remember them though as I have seen them today, descendants of the aurochs as they surely are, stirring an ancient consciousness and waking a memory of a time when all things were wild.

✳

A blaze of blood-red amongst the bracken under the beech trees, a patch of scarlet drawing the eye and halting one's steps with its intensity of colour. I go to look at it, knowing what it must be. Yes, *Amenita muscaria*, the great red toadstool of fairytale picture-books.

Some of the group are already stretched wide - the largest nearly as big as a dinner-plate - others still tight and thrusting as they have come up through the leafy earth-mould, but all are spotted and speckled with white as though some elfin painter had decked them with a white-dipped paintbrush. White spots on a scarlet base: one of Nature's dazzling displays such as an artist would have scarcely dared to invent.

King of the fungi surely it is and holds court amid a host of its kind. When light rain falls on the warm land of late summer, everywhere the earth-children appear. Small pink-gilled heath mushrooms good to eat, bigger horse-mushrooms large as plates, toadstools of crimson, rose-pink, velvet-brown and vermilion, horns of gold and yellow, brackets on branches that elves might sit, splendid shaggy inkcaps in odd places, little brown buttons and fingers of flame amongst the mosses. Bright and beautiful, strange and weird, they come from the underworld to take their share of the sunshine.

Look at them with wonder, for they are wonderful. A

kingdom of life from common earth. Often and again I stop to stare at them. Writers may fantasise, artists imagine, inventing other worlds, but in the end what is more marvellous than the phantasmagoria of the commonplace?

＊

The sound of a mighty rushing of wings. It comes as a muted roar on the evening air, and as it approaches the sky darkens perceptibly. Like a heavy cloud the great flock of starlings passes overhead. Thousand upon thousand there must be, flying in a dark packed mass, homeward bound.

Where do they come from, where do they go? Where they are going to roost this night, I think, are the big fir plantations on the far side of the valley, but where they go to feed in the daytime, I do not really know. A friend told me there are large flocks to be seen on the pastures and plough of the lower country ten or twenty miles away, and certainly it is in this direction I see and hear them setting-off in the early morning, but it seems a long way to go for breakfast. However, with such numbers a vast area must be necessary to sustain them. Sometimes they do pitch around here, filling the trees and covering the ground, and hopefully they eat up a lot of pests.

＊

The birch stands silver-trunked with its feet in the heather and its head in a shower of golden leaves. Slender branches bow down with their cascades of pure gold, and scatter largess like bright coins upon the ground. She is lovely, the Lady of the Forest, as poets have called her, so graceful on a harsh hillside and in company of the more sturdy oaks and beeches.

Yet grace often belies strength, for the birch is immensely hardy and will live where many others will not, and is perhaps the oldest sort of tree to grow upon our hills. Ancestral birches were probably the first real trees to take root in the tundra that followed the retreating ice of the past Ice Age, able to thrive in poor soil and endure intense cold. The birch is still a good coloniser, for whenever a new road-cutting is made, if there is birch in the area, then seedling birches will be the first shrubs to establish themselves in the raw soil.

So look with respect at the graceful sylvan lady when next you see her, for her kind have known the land before all the other trees, and ever man himself set foot upon it.

✳

Another morning at the top of the wood. The country is just passing into autumn: the fern-beds are turning to russet-gold, the leaves are touched to yellow, the heather is sinking into brown although clumps of purple bell-heather still flare royally in a few favoured places. Shafts of sunlight break through the big clouds to light the landscape, but there's an edge to the wind out in the open.

In a sheltered spot under some gorse bushes I sit down to try and sketch, pleased with the glowing colours. Now I am aware of a disturbing sound coming from the depths of the wood, something between a moan, a groan, and a bellow. It sounds like a stag beginning to roar, but it is early days for the rut. There it is again, more definite and nearer. It must be a stag. It is a stag, for with a shake of the leaves he steps into the open.

At first sight he appears a monster, black as a hat. He has been soiling in some patch of liquid peat and all the forepart of him is oozing wet. He eyes glitter from a blackened face, his chin drips with inky-wet, his thick neck-ruff is like a huge black sweep's brush, and black are his lofty antlers. Aware of me, he stops and stares. I remain perfectly still, not quite sure what his intentions are. He makes a circle round me, about twenty yards wide from me, then goes back into the wood again, and I no longer see or hear him.

Soon there will be nightly sounds of roaring or 'bell-ving' hereabouts as the big stags take their stands in diverse places and call the hinds to them for mating. Then by November the rut will be over, and the long winter struggle lie ahead to the spring and the calving.

Roaring Stag.

H.L.B

The golden light of evening gilds the autumn land. I come down the hill to home, gun on one arm and a couple of rabbits swinging from the other hand. Three or four pounds of good wild meat, assured dinners for two or three days. I feel good. My feet rustle the first of the autumn leaves and grass stiffening with frost. I am hungry for my supper. It has been a good day, spent in the open air. I have attended to the needs of livestock, worked in the garden, picked blackberries and stalked round bushes and boundary-hedges like a prehistoric hunter (albeit with different weapon), and now I am coming home with the spoils of the wild, the bounty of nature. I have earned my right to eat meat.

A deep sense of satisfaction, of well-being, is with me. I feel this world is mine, that I am part of it. The hunter is close to Nature. He or she must know all the ways of the wild and have the physical rigour and alertness of the senses necessary to contend with the wilderness and its denizens. He alone meets nature on its own terms and confronts it as an equal.

✳

Sun after rain on the autumn land. The great cleeves, the long slopes, flare with the soaking red bracken of October. Under a stormy sky, caught by the light or plunged into shadow, the fern glows fire-gold like a furnace or sinks to deep mahogany-purple. In the combe and valley bottoms the streams, full with recent rain, run dancing and splashing over their dark stones, twisting and swirling, throwing silver cascades and little water-falls over the rock-ledges, muttering, chattering, singing with the voice of the moor. Between the river and the hill-side the trees assume their own mantle of colour. Oaks hold golden-headed canopy above jet-black trunks and branches, beech, not yet at its zenith of colour, flaunts yellow-gold above dark green, thorn trees carry their loads of crimson berries, ash and rowan, bare now, stand silvery amongst their brighter-clad brethren. At their feet the grass is green like a second spring, but spattered with the gold of fallen leaves.

To walk among so much glory is to almost bewilder the senses. Sight and sound are joined by scent as the smell of moss and damp earth and wet leaves - especially the tang of fallen ash-leaves - pervades the air, and as one moves and walks the forms and colours weave and inter-twine and group and regroup in a living kaleidoscope. Out of the wind, the sun is warm on my hands and face.

I scuff my feet in the wayside leaves as I did as a child, and then stand for a few moments on the little grey bridge, leaning on its rough parapet to look at the rushing water, before turning for home. How lavish are the gifts of Nature, how much wonder and glory and delight for so little world-ly cost. Why do people spend so much money and time seeking for the richness of life when it is all around them?

❋

The harsh shriek of the jays carries across the combe from the stand of beech on the far side. I turn, and see for a moment the flash of the wings with the streak of blue, and the insolent crested heads. Whether they are just scolding me for being where I am, or for other more personal reasons, I don't know, but for sure they are up to mischief of some sort.

Handsome devils they are, and like all the corvids they harm other birds' nests and do damage to ground-nesting birds and their young, and are the bane of gamekeepers. However, at this time of year they will be mainly after nuts and fruits, so I can forgive them and take pleasure in their presence, for their cry is part of the wild world and I would not be without it.

✳

A late October morning on the high moor. Great clouds, white-topped and indigo-bellied, tower up into a cerulean sky, driven by a bitter north-west wind from the sea. The land lies wide beneath, heaving hills and half-hidden valleys, seeming infinite in its loneliness. For here are no homesteads, little even of heather or scrub, only the occasional old boundary-banks, crested with wind-tattered beech, to mark and mould the rise and fall of the land. It is a world of moor-grass and rush, fern and moss and peat-bog.

Across the expanse of sunlit gold, tawny-gold, corn-gold, orange-gold, the cloud-shadows fall, blue and violet, moving and shifting before the strong wind, and down the wind comes the scent of moor and sea.

Far off, so small in space that the human eye can only just mark them, horsemen appear and disappear, riding like men-at-arms in an ancient tale. Somewhere, out of sight and beyond hearing, hounds are hunting. My fingers, half-numb with the raw cold, struggle to hold the field-glasses, buffeted and difficult to focus in the wild weather. The instincts of the hunter are strong.

Now there's a speck on the barren moor, yes, coming nearer and nearer, right towards me. It is the big stag, I see him clearly now, red-bodied, thick-necked, with tall antlers reaching high. On he comes, but not hurrying, just moving at a bouncing trot. Before him is a patch of black peat-bog. He reaches it, and decides to refresh himself by 'soiling' or wallowing in it. He throws himself down and disappears. Then he's up again, and again repeats the process. Finally a heave and a shake, and away somewhere out of sight.

Suddenly the land grows dark. A huge cloud, ink-black, mounts up from the horizon. It overwhelms the scene, then explodes in a blinding hailstorm. I turn about trying to shield my face from the stinging, cutting hail that comes like shot out of the eye of the wind, and struggle down to what shelter I can find. When I can raise my head again, the moor is covered in desolate white and I, despite my heavy clothing, am chilled right through. Thoughts of hot tea by a fireside beckon, so I head for home.

✳

A morning moon. The full round orb hangs lemon-gold in a dusk-blue western sky. Beneath it float wandering clouds, flushed rose-pink by the glow of the rising sun. On the dusky ground below the sheep are rising for the day, held between the two radiances from east and west, and themselves touched by soft yellow and rose. It is like a pastel scene from the hand of a great master. I wish I were skilled enough to paint it myself, but since I am not, I just commit it to memory before it fades.

✳

A late October afternoon. The day is moving towards an early dusk, half-veiled in the misty dampness of autumn, as I come up the e track that curves around the rocky knapp above the river. As I almost reach the top, there, suddenly, are two roe deer, barely twenty yards off. I do not know which of us is most surprised. Possibly I am, for they will have seen people before, whilst I have never seen, nor expected to see, these small, shy, woodland-loving deer on the high and open moor.

How pretty they are, dainty as sprites, two lines of poetry turned to living life! In the seconds of time that we each stand still with surprise, I see the small black-marked muzzles, the dark enquiring eyes, the wing-like ears, the slender limbs, the white-flashed rumps. Then Nature asserts itself and swift action replaces stark surprise. They flee, and as they do so they bound, feet tucked under them, and touch the earth again, stiff-legged, the true capriole leap, and then they are gone, vanished into the scrub below.

I continue on my way, pleased with the unexpected encounter. I had known for a considerable while that roe were returning to the woodlands about the moor, but had not thought to see them hereabouts. Roe are the proper complement to red deer, and co-exist naturally with them. In olden times they were here in the wooded combes, for in 1257 it is recorded that Renold de Mohan, Lord of Dunster, took in the Royal Forest four stags and three roebucks 'by the writ of the Lord King'. At what time, or how or why, the native roe of Exmoor ceased to exist is not known. I wonder what will be the fate of the two roe I have seen today? As my eye did not register antlers, I assume they were either does or young bucks. Probably though, there are others around as yet unseen and unnoticed. I often think that there is more wildlife watching us than ever we ourselves see, and hope that it may be so.

✳

A drumming of hooves, shouting, and the cracking of whips. The galloping herd of ponies comes over the hill, heading for the goyle and plunging downwards. Little wild horses, black manes flying above bay-brown bodies, tails streaming in the wind, they pour into the rocky cleft at top speed in a way no ordinary horse would dare, sure-footed as mountain goats, knowing every step of the terrain as a deer would know it.

The horsemen riding behind swing outwards,

choosing an easier way down, knowing the ponies will head for the river-crossing. For this is the day of the autumn drift, or pony-gathering, and the men of the moor, like the ponies, know the way of things.

Now the herd is out of the goyle and pounding through the rushes towards the river. The outriders make haste to keep on the flanks lest any of the ponies try to break away. The river-bank is reached, and the little horses plunge through the ford, churning the water and sending the spray flying high. Over and up now, away over the moor, through the heather and bracken, wild things in a wild land.

Watching, I have seen what prehistoric man would have seen: wild horses fleeing as from their natural enemies. Then both wolves and men would have hunted them for meat; now, however, they are being gathered for parting-out, sorting, and the branding of foals. When they reach the holding fields on the far side of the hill, they will be parted according to brand and taken to the respective home-farms for a few days. Then most of them, those not required for sale, will be returned to the moor again.

They are over the skyline now, out of sight, with the last of the rearguard riders just struggling after them. The moor seems empty without them. Like the deer they are part of the land. By their presence one is drawn to an older world.

H . L . B .

The little stream under the bog runs vermilion-red. Its hurrying water ripples round its stones with seemingly unnatural colour, as though red-ochre had been poured into it.

Which is exactly what has happened. It is red with bog-iron, iron oxide, iron leached from the soil and rock. I know very little about the phenomenon, but it occurs in many of the high-ground springs, and colours the margins of lower rivers too, usually in autumn. Looking at my stream now, I can readily understand old lore speaking of 'rivers running with blood'.

Iron is good for one, so I decide to drink some. It is bitter tasting, like sucking rusty nails. Surely it would be beneficial to someone suffering from anaemia? I wonder if anyone has ever thought of that? Perhaps a fortune might be made by bottling some of it!

❊

Moonlight. How bright is an October or November moon! I have often observed this to be so. Its light seems stronger and brighter than at other times. As I walk now across the little bridge, its clear brilliance sets the water of the river glittering like shattered glass and sheds white radiance across the grassy mead beyond, and bathes the upper hillside. The floor of the lane is a pool of silver barred with the black shadows of trees, and the sky is velvet-dark. The voice of an owl carries on the air sharp with autumn frost.

To my right-hand the moonlight touches the withy-grown marsh but does not penetrate it. The thicket of trees holds darkness, depths and deep places into which the eye of the moon cannot peer. I feel some curious stirring within myself, part expectancy, part apprehension, as I pass by, I know not why. The tales of Grendal and Forfar seem very real and very near. I am sure a dragon dwells in the dark and hidden hollows of the carr. I expect to see his eyes of green fire look out at me and hear the sound of a scaly body uncoiling amongst the rushes.

I am glad to be nearly home. Do not mock, this is an ancient land, and not even science can banish beliefs and responses of a thousand years and more. Moonlight casts mystery with its shadows, and who shall say what we perceive, or how, or why.

❋

The sound of the horn echoes up the valley. I sit by the rocks and wait. The sun is warm after the frosty night, the sky a duck's-egg blue above a tawny landscape and the river twists in silver flows below.

Hounds are drawing the river-banks and the fir plantations on the far side. The huntsman's coat shows a splash of red above the dark cover and riders appear and disappear wraith-like along the hedge at the rim of the cleeve. On the shoulder of the hill to my left horsemen wait in a group, as low down the precipitous slope as they dare to go, watchers

H.L.B

The Shadow of the Great Cleeve

in the fern and bush, motionless except for the toss of a horse's head or the flick of a tail, the eye called to them by one grey mount like a chieftain's charger in the midst.

The fox, big, old and cunning is loath to move, but the huntsman cheers his hounds on with horn and voice. Thirty lambs were killed at the farm above this past spring, and the killer and his kind must be called to account.

A hound speaks, then the pack takes it up, a great cry ringing and echoing through the cover and from side to side of the valley and up to the hills. Excitement courses through blood and brain, tingling up through my scalp. There's a holloa at the top of the wood and out for the moor he goes! Now the red rover must run for his life!

The horsemen on the hill have gone, down some hidden paths to the river-crossing, and the cleeve is as though they had never been, or phantoms from another age. Now I must go home, for there is much to do about farm and garden these shortening days.

✳

November, and the beech trees blaze like the last flames of a sinking fire, furnace-red in the morning light. The night's rain has served to intensify the colour and the grey cloud and half-mist accentuates its depth and fierceness. Orange-red, flame-red, deep crimson-red, dark-purple shadows held in the leafy depths, the hills behind violet-grey, emerald grass below: the colour almost overwhelms the eye. Yet even as a fierce fire burns itself out, as the beech-leaves reach their zenith of colour, so they begin to fall. Already those trees on the windward end of the stand show stark black boughs through the veil of fire, and stand with their feet in drifts of russet and green moss.

Soon all the leaves will be down and the branches bare and black. All that is except on the very young trees and close-cropped hedges. For it is a peculiarity of the beech that in infancy it does not shed its summer leaves until the following spring, when they are pushed-off by the freshly-opened buds. I can only suppose that this is because the old thick leaves give a measure of protection to young growth. (Spring leaves, just breaking from the bud are in fact very tender and can be cruelly damaged by late frost, so that a severe shock can be given to youthful twigs). Once the tree has arrived at a fairly mature state, strong and resilient, it no doubt feels it can dispense with this mechanism.

Now I must make haste to finish my small sketch, for later the weather may change, and even tomorrow more leaves will be down. So reach for the burnt-sienna, vermilion, crimson and cobalt, cadmium, viridian and black - at no other time will I need them as now!

✳

I've just brought in some trails of ivy to add to my jar of now rather sparse late-autumn flowers. These will help to eke-out the home decoration until the time comes to bring in the holly and fir for Christmas, 'The Holly and the Ivy....' The glossy dark green leaves of both are ever to hand in winter when all around the trees, save only the conifers, are bare and the garden bereft of flowers.

How splendidly decorative is the ivy! Every leaf is a perfect pattern, each trail can be flexed to suit your wishes. One of the commonest things that grows, it is one of the most beautiful. I never tire of looking at its leaf-forms, and when I was young and had more time, I used to draw the various shapes, or press them in a book.

Hereabouts ivy grows everywhere - everywhere that is, where there is reasonable shelter, for I have observed it does not like a high exposed position - covering old banks, clinging to walls, and climbing up into trees.

Concerning its habit of climbing up trees, I have also observed that it has a particular preference for ash and thorn, but no liking for beech. All three sorts of tree grow closely in the hedges here, but whereas the ivy will do its best to scramble up the two former, the latter it leaves well alone. Why this should be I do not know. Nor do I know to what extent it damages trees. It makes a heavy mop-head in the thorns, but as these seem to survive alright, putting forth masses of May blossom every summer, and as the birds find shelter amongst the ever-green leaves in winter, on the whole I leave it alone.

Nor have I ever made up my mind whether the great variation in leaf-form is due to distinct varieties (botanists say there is only one species, *Hedera helix*) or simply to variable growth-habit. I have noticed that some ivies will start-off near the ground with one sort of leaf, then change the fashion as they rise up in the world (as does the holly, changing its prickly leaves to smooth). One particular ivy plant though, that I know of, always garbs itself with unvarying leaves of most beautiful form, long-fingered almost like Virginia creeper. I have several times tried to grow a cutting from it, but so far have not succeeded.

*

Rain, and a thickening wet mist driving down off the hills on a sou'west wind. I struggle round with the chores, cursing the mud that comes up to the tops of my boots as I feed the cattle, also the rain that manages to run down inside the collar of my raincoat and up the cuffs as well. I think how nice it will be when I can go indoors and have my hot cup of coffee.

Suddenly, out of the mist comes the cry of hounds. With equal suddenness all thoughts of home comfort vanish. Now I see them. They are racing down the cleeve, and their wild cry fills the combe. There is no-one with them, they must have run right away from their huntsman, the whole pack hunting a fox on their own. For a ,moment they check by the stream, then cast themselves. It is wonderful to see them turning this way and that, mud-dark, questing almost to my feet.

Now they have it again, they are off across the lane and up over the Ball. Their voices fade away as they head out across the fields for the cleeves of the River Barle, then they are gone as suddenly as they came. It has been like watching the passing of the Wild Hunt of ancient legend, and the excitement of it remains with me.

Later a few horsemen appear in the grey landscape, dark with rain, and the huntsman himself, his red coat sodden to a dull crimson. Then they too are gone. I come in and have my coffee.

❋

Red dawn. All the eastern sky is an arc of fierce glowing crimson. It is as though the heavens are on fire, as though a furnace burns beyond the rim of the purple-dark hills. The black branches of the trees are like a charcoal drawing across the face of the infinite.

'Red sky at dawning, shepherd's warning', says the old tag, for a red morning light has long been held to presage violent weather. Why, I do not know, though wind and rain do seem often to follow after. Conversely, a fiery sunset is thought to be a good sign: 'Red sky at night, shepherd's delight'. So sheep may rest in peace through a calm night, or so it is hoped.

Now the furnace-sky is subsiding into gold, and soon the sun will be up, and I must put aside my pencil and start the day's chores.

The tawny-owls are nosiy tonight. The resident-pair in the old beech tree are vociferous in the moonlight. 'Tu-wit, tu-wit' says one, 'Hoo-hoo-hoo' says the other.

I seldom see them, they are voices of the night. Once though, I did have a remarkable view of one of them, in broad daylight. During a summer afternoon my attention was called to a lot of blackbird chatter in a tree behind the barn, and suddenly a chestnut-brown owl flew out in a great hurry, pursued by a pair of irate blackbirds.

One of the two, the cock, harried the owl across the combe, almost hanging on to his - or her - tail, and did not give up the chase until Tawny was well away. It was rather like seeing a terrier chasing a bullock!

I guess the blackbirds had suspected the owl of having an untoward interest in their nest thereabouts, and therefore had 'seen him off'.

✳

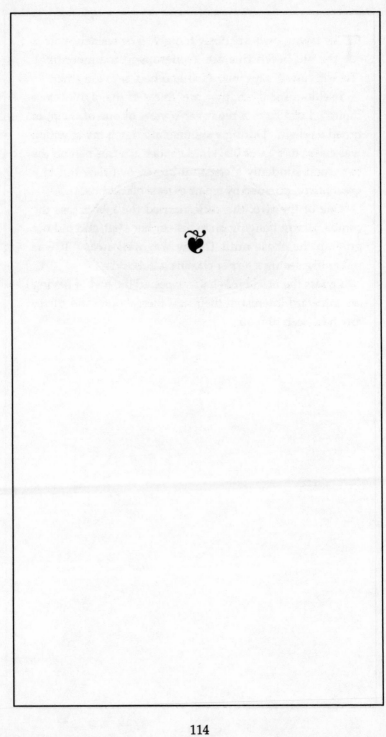

WINTER

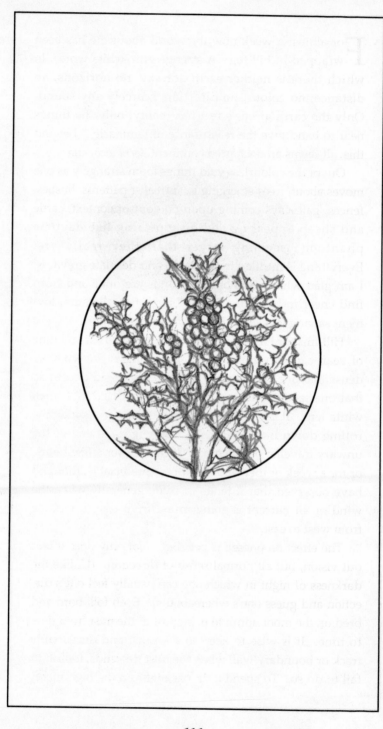

For almost a week now the world about me has been wrapped in hill-fog. A strange grey-white world, in which there is neither earth nor sky, no horizons, no distance, no colour, no direction, scarcely any sound. Only the earth at one's feet has reality, only the things near to hand give the reassurance of familiarity. Beyond this, all seems an uncharted continent, *terra incognita*.

Out of the colourless void things loom strangely as one moves about, trees emerging in surrealist patterns, bushes, fences, gateways coming upon one out of context, cattle and sheep appearing and disappearing like daytime phantoms, seeming larger than they really are. Everything is muffled in the damp and desolate greyness. I am glad when my morning rounds are done and I can find cheer in hot coffee and a bright fire, then employment sawing logs in the barn for evening comfort.

Hill-mist or hill-fog is curious. It can occur at any time of year, can vary in thickness, becoming at the worst so dense that one can only see a few yards round oneself so that one seems to be moving about enveloped in a small white tent. It can settle gradually, or descend suddenly, rolling down like cloud from the heights to engulf the unwary traveller on the moor. It can last for a few hours, or for a week or thereabouts. It is unpredictable, though I have observed that it tends to come generally when the wind or air current is going round from east to west or from west to east.

The effect on oneself is peculiar. Not only does it blot out vision, but all normal sense of direction. (Unlike the darkness of night in which one can usually feel one's direction and guess one's whereabouts). Even folk born and bred on the moor admit to being lost in the mist from time to time. It is wise to keep to a known and discernable track or boundary-wall when the mist descends, foolish to fail to do so. To spend a day or night on the high moor, stumbling around in the cold and dark, is not pleasant, and the chance of blundering into a bog even more unpleasant, and possibly dangerous. If caught unawares by the sudden descent of hill-fog, the most sensible thing to do is to go downhill, because the mist is always less dense in the valleys than on the hilltops, also by following a stream downwards along its course, one is bound to come eventually to a bridge, a road, and to habitation.

✳

A winter morning, bare black trees and red fern and sear dun grass underfoot, but there's a rift of blue sky in the clouds above as I climb to the top of the hill. Suddenly, a drumming of hooves, a rushing of bodies through the bracken, and a herd of deer comes up over the rise before me. Something has set them running, and heedless of me they cross my line of approach not many yards ahead. Some thirty stags, close grouped, dark against the light and in their winter coats, antlered heads held high. A few moments and they are over the brow and sinking the far side of the hill, another moment and only their antlers show above the sky line, then they are gone.

A tingling of excitement still courses through me, a primeval stirring. For a moment I have stood in an ancient world, a world where all things are wild, and man a hunter for his meat. More than any other creatures, deer express and awaken the spirit of the wilderness and rouse the atavistic instinct that lies below the surface of ourselves.

'The running of the deer.' A line set in a Christmas carol speaks of older things, and the roots of life far off in time and beginnings long ago.

✳

Someone asked me the other day, did I believe in the Beast of Exmoor? I answered yes. This seemed to surprise them.

I base my premise on, firstly, that there is no reason why it should not exist. Until an Act of 1976 forbade the keeping of exotic and potentially dangertous wild animals except under licence, anyone could, almost literally, keep a lion in the backyard or an alligator in the bath. When such possession became illegal, some persons turned their erstwhile 'pets' loose to survive how they could, or die, as the case might be. Add to this the fact that the small private zoos of the time often did not have very good security arrangements, and sometimes animals escaped. Thus, all sorts of strange animals have turned up in the English countryside - porcupines in a Devon woodland, arctic foxes near Bristol and, reputedly, a monkey in Culbone woods!

A big cat, puma, panther or cheetah, could survive very well in an area such as this, once it got used to killing for its supper. An abundance of sheep and deer, the occasional calf or foal (such losses, unexplained, have occurred from time to time), plus plenty of rabbits to fill any hungry gaps, would supply its bodily needs, whilst deep valleys choked with scrub and woodland would give it the cover necessary to its security and survival, protection from the enemy Man.

Assuming it to be a dark melanistic puma, which seems to be the most favoured identity, a person would be most unlikely to see it except by chance. The puma is a creature shy of human beings, and does its best to avoid them. Some years ago I spent a while with friends on Vancouver Island, where the population of pumas or cougars is greater per given area than anywhere else in the Americas, and we were out in the bush every day, but never saw one of these creatures. Now-and-again my friend's husband, who was a hunter, would point to some sign which his practised eye could see, and say 'cat'. They were around and no doubt watching us, though we could not see them.

Another pointer to the Exmoor killer being a feline and not a dog or a large black fox (melanistic foxes have been known to occur) as some folk say, is the manner of the killing, also the fact that no pack of foxhounds has been able to fluish it out of cover, even when it was almost certainly there. The killings of which I have been shown photographs by the friends and neighbours with whom I have talked, are made, and the meat consumed, in a manner not like that of a dog. Also the killer is silent. I have had, unfortunately, direct experience of sheep-worrying dogs, and they are always noisy, and tend to attack the sheep from behind.

Regarding the beating or drawing of cover, any dog would be driven out - sheep-killing dogs are always eventually themselves killed - but pussy will go up a tree, and in the drakness of a plantation who can see a black cat up a Christmas tree? As to hounds, hounds will only speak to the quarry they are entered-to, and foxhounds would not bay a cat up a tree. For this one would need cougar-hounds from the other side of the Atlantic.

Something else seems by now obvious; that there must be, and have been, more than one of these creatures. The length of time since the killings first started, up to the most recent attacks, is now too great for the effective life-time of any one beast. So we are left with the assumption that the original escapee was a pregant female, or that there was from the beginning more than one beast and that they have bred.

Which brings one to the matter of species and breed-ings and the possibility of hybrids. It is just possible that the beast and its kind could be a cross between some other escaped cat-creature and a feral domestic cat - hybrids are often larger than either parent. Unless and until someone traps or shoots such a creature, we can only guess.

One thing more though there is to be told: within living memory - that is, the memory of an elderly farmer who has lived all his life on a farm near Withypool - there were wildcats living amongst the rocks on the precipitous cleeves of Room Hill above the River Exe. A man of marvellous memory, he once described to me, in great detail, one he had seen when a small boy. From this description, I have little doubt that here survived, most remarkably, a last remnant of *Felis sylvestris* .* These fierce wild cats became extinct sometime round-about the years of the First World War, no doubt trapped or shot-out by local farmers.

Dare one wonder if just a very few of these cats did survive for long enough for a last one to meet and mate with something escaped from a zoo? We shall never know.

* see *Living on Exmoor*

The Hill of the Cats.

H.L.B.

A wet day on the moor. Pouring rain from morning to night, driving, dripping, splashing, a misery to man and beast. Wet black heather, squelching black peat, soaking brown-dun rush, no colour but sodden brown-red fern, no sound but the beating of rain and the moaning of the wind. Lead-grey clouds lie low on lead-grey hills so that the one can scarce be distinguished from the other, and the world seems dissolved in a primal greyness.

What can one do on a day like this? Birds and beasts have common sense, and are tucked away in what shelter they can find. Nothing moves on the moor. One should follow Nature's wisdom. Thoughts of a cosy home, a bright fire, and hot coffee call one down from the hills. It is time to go.

✳

The cavalcade comes down to the ford of the river, brushing through the dark wet heather and sodden fern. The river runs high with the recent rain, itself galloping over its rocks and boulders, silver maned above its depths, its voice the voice of a river-god.

It is no easy crossing. The huntsman comes first, his horse plunging in up to its girth, his coat vivid above the steel-dark foam-crusted water, calling the hounds to follow him. They come, and are swimming now, heads above the foam. Together they gain the far bank, and a hundred horsemen follow them. Rider after rider, in showers of flying spray, until they are all across and rising the opposing hill and are gone away.

The ford is lonely again. It has known many such passages, and sometimes there have been casualties. The river is strong when running in spate, and horses have been swept off their feet. Even smaller fords of lesser rivers have drowned human beings. Only in company should such a passage be attempted, for indeed a vengeful god seems to lie in the river, waiting to reassert the power of Nature with the snatching of a sacrificial victim.

Yet, if fast to rise the hill-country waters are quick to subside, and tomorrow, or the day after, the river may be just a jolly stream again.

✳

Frost, and all the world lies silver under a sky of ducks'-egg blue. As the sun peers over the hill all things sparkle in the clear light. The grass of the valley rustles under my feet and the air is sharp. Everywhere the hoar-frost decks each blade of grass and spire of rush, each twig or strand of wire in a fence, every stone and stick with its rime of silvery-white. Here in a nook, as yet untrampled, rise last year's grass heads, each a marvel of silver filigree, and amongst them spiders' webs woven of silver thread. I kneel down the better to look at them. The exquisite beauty of little things.

The breath of the sun is stronger now, and its warmth begins to fill the valley. A blackbird sings to the golden light, and the fairy world dissolves like a dream, leaving only a memory.

✳

The bare winter thorn trees stand black against the red winter sunset, they are twisted and gnarled and crouching, for they have struggled for life in a ruthless world. The strife of years and a hundred gales has battered and torn at them. The salt sea wind has flayed them, the rain has drenched them, the drought has shrivelled them, the frost has bitten them, the hungry beasts of the moor have snapped and gnawed at them, yet they live defiant, clasping at the thin acid soils with their roots and lifting their tattered heads to the sun.

I walk up to them through the heather, stand with my

feet in the puddled hollow made by countless sheep circling and rubbing against the trunks, and touch the rough black bark of one of them. Does a spirit live within? The ancients believed so. Surely some presence resides herein, giving strength and life-force to such grim existence. No other sort of tree could face conditions on the high bare windswept moor and survive.

The red sky is sinking now into nightfall. Soon it will be dark and bitter cold take hold. Time to hurry home now, but as I do I turn to look once more at the valiant little trees, their twisted branches a pattern against the hollowness of space, and salute them before I go.

❋

The bitter wind of December blows hard out of the north-west, bearing with it bursts of hail or stinging rain from the dark clouds above. Along the edge of the moor, in the partial shelter of a gorse-grown wind battered beech-fence, a file of ponies moves. Were it not for the movement, I would hardly see them, so much a part of the moor are they, the bay and brown of their bodies is the colour of the winter bracken, the black of their points matches the dormant heather, the mealy dun of their underparts is the exact shade of the bleached rush and sear moor-grass. Only their almost flour-white mealy noses stand out from the natural harmony of body and herbage and catch the eye.

A long winter, inevitably a hard one, perhaps one of deep snow and ice and bitter cold, is before them. Yet they will survive as wild animals survive. Nature has equipped them to be part of this harshland. Their coats, so fine and glossy in the summer, are now bear-thick, and hard on the surface like those of deer. Rain and hail and snow will be shed as off a roof. The abundant manes will protect eyes and ears, tails with a brush-like thickness near the dock will tuck into more sensitive hinder parts. Strong jaws will crunch the hard winter vegetation of the moor and the tips of anything that protrudes above the snow and ice. Wide nostrils will inhale the bitterest air, and long deep wind-pipes convey it softened to the lungs. Strong bones and sound hoofs will carry them through snowdrifts and over sheets of ice. When everything is snowbound and every scrap of surface moisture frozen hard, they will mouth the snow or crack the ice with their hooves for water. They will live where sheep and cattle perish. Only the wild red deer can match them in hardiness.

They are way-wise too. They know the hollows that hold the winter sunshine, the goyles and combes that give shelter according as the wind blows. Searching for graz-ing in the open, they will drift before the wind with tails tucked in - until the strengthening wind proclaims a storm, when they will turn and walk into it, knowing that only by moving up-wind will they find a bank or wall that will give them the wind break that they need.

So I leave them now and face the weather myself to gain the shelter of the lane.

✳

A sky of pure glowing gold above a world of silver-blue. A winter dawn, with all the land frost-bound and all things stiff with cold. The frozen grass is crisp under my feet and rustles with each step. The sheep lie still, not anxious to rise from their night's bedding.

The golden light grows more intense, the rim of the hills darkens now against it, I feel a moment of waiting, then, behold, the sun like an opening eye peers over the horizon and reaches to me with dazzling rays. The river in the valley below takes up the rays and reflects them back to the heavens, becoming a ribbon of rippling gold and silver among the bare dark withies and alders.

The sheep begin to rise now, leaving patches of green where their warm bodies have kept the frost from the earth. I turn and go further down the valley, under the line of beech trees. As the sun mounts up the trees in its path cast long blue shadows over the silvery ground. I can feel the warmth on my face now. By the time I get home I shall be quite hot - but that mug of hot coffee will be welcome just the same!

✳

Cold moonlight on a cold world. Silver frost and black shadows and strange patterns on the earth, and all is still.

Out of the darkness, down the alleys of the night, comes a wailing, a weird cry rising and falling, sobbing like that of a soul in torment. It is coming nearer, and if I did not know what it was, my 'hair would stand on end.' The banshee is a vixen calling for her lover,

H L B

View through the Gap

She subsides for a little, then clear and staccato from the hill comes the answering bark of the dog-fox. There is dominance in the call, something that speaks for the land under the trees, under the gorse and fern. The voice of the wild. There's a warning in it to the lesser creatures of life, and I'm glad my bantams are safely housed.

I stand for a moment feeling myself part of this wild world, then return indoors.

✳

The dead sheep, or what is left of it, lies amongst the tussocks. A bloody mess, with scattered wool all around, eyes gone, belly split and guts pulled out, bones cracked and gnawed. What ailed it, I do not know, but probably it got lodged on its back whilst rolling, and heavy in wool, could not rise again - a common occurrence on the moor.

It would not have died easily. A sheep on its back will last several hours before death comes naturally. But the predators and carrion-eaters do not wait. Ravens, crows and magpies circling overhead see the prize and come for the feast. First they gouge out the eyes, then tear out the tongue, then they split the belly for the tit-bits inside. Then come the foxes and badgers and finish the disembowling and rend the carcase apart and glut themselves on meat. At what stage of the butchery the life of the wretched victim is extinguished, no one knows. It is one of the many cruelties of the hill-country.

Why do I tell you this? So that you may know the moor as I know it. Why do strangers glibly use the words beauty, peace, harmony of Nature? Beauty, yes, there is great beauty and wonder in all the land, and in small things too, more than the hand or mind of Man could ever fashion by artifice, but peace, no, there is only strife, and the harmony is but that of utter ruthlessness.

Everything in the world of wild Nature is cruel and without mercy. Everything survives by preying on something else. The fox kills what it can, often to excess, and so does the stoat, the owl and the hawk. The pretty merlin takes a toll of some 400 small birds each year. The grey squirrel eats the little nestling birds alive, and so does the handsome magpie. The crow swallows the chicks of pheasant and partridge. The dragonfly sitting on a twig by my garden fence snatches an inoffensive little insect from a leaf, and I hear the crunch as it consumes it head-first. Even the fine handsome plant that you notice and admire is as it is because it has choked-out its neighbours.

The wilderness is a violent place. In it the weak and faint-hearted will not survive.

✳

A branch from the old thorn bush has blown down in the night. As I pick it up to cast out of my way, I marvel at all the lichens that encrust it in festoons of pale grey-green. So many sorts: some in fluffy masses, some in close clusters, some like miniature bushes themselves, some like pendant streamers. Like an aerial garden planted by elves. In sober fact, they are testimony to the wet humid climate of the combes.

Collectively, they seem to have acquired the name 'Spanish Moss', though what Spaniards may have to do with this, I don't know. Possibly someone once saw a likeness to the hoary decking of trees in the Florida swamps. Anyway, twigs so garnished make good adjuncts to winter dried-flower-and-leaf arrangements when there is little else to fill the vases.

✳

Here I sit on a cold winter afternoon amongst the rocks of a favourite place in the middlemost part of my valley. Before me the river runs steel-blue, crested with silver, full and strong, coming down from its source on high Exmoor. It is fierce and noisy, alone in its winter valley, tumbling over rock-ledge and foaming about black boulders, swirling dark in its deeper pools. Overhead the sky is a cold pale blue. The sun, low now, gilds all one side of the valley, touching the bracken-tangled hills to ruddy gold, and its light is warm on my face. On the far side, where the day's sun has not touched at all, the great hollow north-facing cleeves are plunged into deep blue shadow, and the frost-bound ground is set like iron, dappled with frozen sleet, and every hag and hoof-hole filled with white ice. A few black withies fringe the river-bank amidst brown rushes. High up, where hardy rowans and one or two witch-like-thorns cling to the precipitous hillside, some hill-sheep graze. They are the only life here at the moment, save myself.

Though the valley today may seem untenanted, at another time I might see all sorts of wild creatures and buzzards soaring on great moth-like wings, a kestrel hovering as though suspended from the heavens on a thread, perhaps a peregrine scything the air, a pair of harriers passing this way, ravens 'talking' with their guttural voices, a heron fishing in the river. Deer perhaps in the sheltered combe that breaks from the west, a prowling fox, a stoat peering from a cleft, a badger foraging, maybe an adder, and many a lesser creature of the insect world.

The sun draws low to the rim of the big cleeves, turning them to a darker blue. The whole valley is in shadow now, and I feel the bitter cold of evening beginning to take hold. It is time to go.

The ice splinters under my feet and I walk carefully over the rigid ground lest I do my ankles a mischief.

Then I stop for a moment and turn for a last look up the valley. Suddenly it is timeless, I seem to see other beasts, other things, than I have seen in the daylight. Thicker scrub on the hillsides, a lordly elk moving through the withy-beds, the shadow of a wolf before the rising moon. And that dark shape behind the rocks - is it a bear? Movement in the bushes - lynx or wild cat? Is that the grunt of a wild boar in the bottom of the little combe? The cattle I see huge and dark on a patch of river-marsh, are they aurochs or bison? It matters not, for once all were here, before Man decimated his inheritance. There are other Presences too: hunters going home, their spoils upon their shoulders, their spearheads points of light. A wizard making magic in the hollow. What else? It is no time to stand about. My cosy home calls to me. I hurry on now, as quickly as I am able, to be indoors before nightfall.

In the dusk I hear the sudden gabbling of wild duck, then the heavier movement of ponies disturbed by my sudden approach. At least they are real enough. The little wild horses of Exmoor, they belong to past and present alike, linking the yesterday's prehistory with this winter evening, this moment of *now*. So I go up the hill to home and another day is gone to join all the others that have sped before it.

✳

'The holly bears a berry as red as any blood...' and so does this dark December day. The holly tree at the top of the wood on the precipitous cleeve bears a load of scarlet such as one would scarcely believe were it painted in a picture.

It is a tall tree, full-grown, and rises high above my head, holding its crown of splendour brilliant against the grey sky of the shortening winter afternoon. No bush ever bred or cultivated by Man the gardener can match the wild holly for the profusion and spectrum-redness of its berries, nor does any other tree set off its fruits with such massed deep-green shining foliage. As I look up at the beautiful tree that rises so royally here in the depth of the winter, amongst the bare-branched thorns and scrub-oaks, I notice what a clever tree it is: up to a height of about seven or eight feet it bears the needle-spined prickly leaves we know so well; above this height, the approximate limit of animal browsing, it dispenses with such armament and grows only plain smooth leaves. How many generations of trial-and-error, of natural selection, have taught it this ploy? I speak with respect to her - it is a she-tree, for only the female bears the berries - and take just a few sprigs for my Christmas decoration.

There are many hollies in various states of growth, in and about this and other woods, and in the hedge-banks, for the holly is a native tree in these parts, growing naturally in company with oak, ash and hazel. Testimony to this is given by a number of places having received the name of Homebush, holm or home being the ancient name for holly, no doubt once prolific in these parts.

*

A grey winter's day, and the wind coming down from the moor buffets the trees in the valley. The river runs cold as I walk along its margin. There is little of life to be seen, but from afar there comes a call like a promise.

Somewhere a mistle-thrush is singing. Loud as a blackbird and clear as a bugle, his beautiful notes come down the wind. High in swaying black branches he challenges the winter and calls to the spring. Stormcock is the name that has been given him, for he sings in wild weather, the only bird to sing in the winter.

He is our thrush of the hills, dwelling and nesting where the gentler song-thrush of the meadows does not care to come. He and his mate are strong birds, with leopard-spotted breasts, and not always as shy as one might think, for once I had a pair nest in the corner of a windowsill, and raise a family there.

✳

All day long the snow has fallen, softly, quietly, without wind or sound. Now, with nightfall, the snow is ceasing, the clouds drifting away, and a full round moon looks down on a scene of unearthly beauty. Like a child filled with wonder, I decide to go for a walk.

The snow is soft underfoot, but even for there has been no drifting. As I walk this way and that, down to the river and up to the hill and back again, I step into an enchanted world. The moon is a lamp in a velvet sky of black, the earth a realm of silver white, and all around the trees stand laden with fresh snow-blossom, it is as though every tree, every bush, had put forth white flowers on every branch and every twig. The summer of a snow-queen, a fantasy of dreams.

Barred shadows cross my feet, the lotus-bloom is over my head, there is no movement but my own, no sound of any sort. It is a night of magic, with all things bound by some unreal spell. The trees I see by day have another guise, proclaim another dimension. Shall I wake up, and into what world shall I wake?

I find my way home again, and so to bed. Morning now, and rain has washed away my dream-flowers. Only a memory remains.

A scatter of torn ivy in the snowbound lane. Looking up, I see the ivy bush on the old thorn-trees has been nibbled to about head height, and I guess the creature responsible, then, looking down I see the slots. They are smallish, and freshly made. A hind, and she is not far off. At the bend of the lane I see her. Winter-brown, her coat thick and dark in the snowy world, she seems to be alone, for I do not see others. Nor does she seem to have a calf with her. Perhaps she is old, a yeld hind, but it is difficult to tell.

For a minute she looks at me, then disappears through a gap in the hedge, seeming to melt away in the curious way that deer do vanish. I hope she will find enough sustenance until better times return. Winter is a hard time for the wild things, but deer survive on many pickings, nibbling ivy, holly, and the tips of anything that protrudes above snow and ice. And of course they will raid the root-fields of the hill farms, often doing much damage, especially to turnips.

❊

F ox-tracks in the snow. Onwards they run, sometimes in a straight line, sometimes turning hither and thither as something catches the attention of the maker, but never seeming to stop. He - I assume it is a dog-fox as the prints are fairly large - runs single-footed, each footfall touching the snow in exact alignment, and equidistant, as though printed by mechanical means.

The footprints pass through a gateway, and so do I, and there he is crossing the next field. He is a dark sharp-cut figure, almost black against the hollow whiteness of the snow. Lean, long-legged and wolfish, he is unlike the pretty cat-like beast of the picture books. Your hill-country fox is big of his kind, a hunter and a killer. Life in time of deep snow or iron-bound frost is hard, and he takes what he can get, raiding the farmyard by night, or even by day if the human guardian is elsewhere. A strong fox will tear inch-thick planking from a hen-house, or, if the ground below the snow is not frozen hard, burrow down and come up through the floor. If it is lambing-time then he will take a lamb a night. Even the unwary homestead cat may be snapped-up.

I half-raise the gun, then lower it. He is almost out of range and entering some gorse bushes. I cannot be sure of a clean shot. I do not like shooting foxes. More shot foxes go away wounded, with smashed limbs, to die a wretched lingering death from starvation and gangrene, than are killed outright.

So Charlie goes free this time, but he'd better not let me see him near my home, or he'll not get a second chance.

✳

Glass frost. One step outside my door and I go down on the flat of my back with the soles of my feet up to heaven. The next thing is to get up. Easier said than done. Each attempt results in going down whack again. However, I do at last get back indoors and then re-emerge with a panfull of fire-ash to strew in front of my feet, and so cross the skating-rink that is the yard and get to the barn where the tools lie. Then, 'digger' in hand, I set out to chop little paths in the ice-sheet to wherever I need to go.

Gradually I work my way out onto the Ball and look around. The whole world roundabout is one of dazzling white frozen snow, shining and glistening like a polished mirror in the morning sun. The ground is sheet-ice, the branches of trees, and all things projecting above ground-level, are coated to many times their own thickness with glittering ice as though molten glass had been poured over them. I call the sheep, as I have a bag of cake for them, and they come, or try to come, stiff-legged as though they were on skates. This way and that they skid, tobogganing and colliding on the glass-like surface. The dodgems at Barnstaple Fair come a good second!

On the way back I make an error: a sideways step to look into the combe. My feet are gone from me and I'm skidding down the precipitous slope on my back! Faster and faster, and I know there's a line of withies at the bottom by the stream. If I crack against them at the speed I'm going, I'll do myself an injury. Desperately I manage to roll over and try to clutch at whatever protrudes - gorse and brambles and the like - above the ice, and manage to come to a reasonable stop by the withies. Next, how do I get back up? Directly is impossible, so I work my way down the combe till I meet the junction with the lane, then haul myself homewards by the hedge. Am thankful to be back with a mug of hot tea in my hands!

Glass frost can occur in one of two ways: a partial thaw after snow, followed by a sudden severe frost (as now) or by heavy rain suddenly freezing. I have known both, and in the latter case, many years ago now, sheep were frozen to the ground and had to be helped up.

❋

Blizzard. For three days and three nights the snow has come out of the east on a howling wind. It comes now with terrible elemental force, battering, blinding, tearing, choking, the sky is gone, the moor is blotted out, there is nothing but snow between heaven and earth.

Trees and hedges bend before the fury. Wherever there is a gap or gateway, the snow blows through in great white clouds. Everywhere the drifts mount up and up, smoking at the tops like volcanos. Up to the hedges, over the gates, up to the eves of buildings, over the shoulders of combes. Every hollow is filled, every lane choked to the top of its banks. And still it snows.

I stay close to the buildings, carrying a spade to dig my way where I must, then move along to the lee-side of the hedge-banks to get to the small field at the back of the barn where the ewes abide. They are huddled in the middle, heads and backs above the snow. Hopefully they will stay there and not bury. They have the windbreak of three tall beech hedges which should hold back the full force of the blizzard somewhat. The danger is if they draw too much to the shelter of the lee-side, for it is here, by the bitter irony of Nature, that the drifts grow deepest and highest, it is here that sheep bury.

I am glad to come down again, back to the life-saving comfort of home and warmth. It is like the return to port from a ferocious sea. Beyond the enclosing harbour of walls and windbreaks the storm is impossible to face. It comes at you like a moving wall of white. You cannot see through it, cannot look into it. It cuts off your breath with its icy cold and stifles you. You cannot walk, the ever-mounting snow muffles your feet. Woe to the traveller lost on the moor, all land marks gone. Some there are who have not come home.

Where are all the wild things now? Where are the ponies? All things must struggle to survive, how they can, if they can. The ponies like the deer will live, they know where to find shelter enough, how to pick at any vegetation that protrudes above the snow. The lesser creatures, alas, so very many will die. That any will survive at all - as a few always do - seems a miracle.

I do the little that I can. I beat down patches of snow by my door, and crumble and spread whatever I can spare of foodstuff for the birds, (and the hayseed from the bales helps too). So many come. Blackbirds, robins, tits, chaffinches, dunnocks, starlings and a handsome cock pheasant as well. The tiny wrens make my heart ache. They will not pick at the crumbs, or the hayseeds that help the other birds, though they fly into the barn in the hope of insects in the crevices.

Beyond this, I can only pray, for myself, the animals and the birds, and hope the blizzard will blow itself out soon.

✳

Rain beating down from a leaden sky, washing away the snow of February. The moor lies dark and black, sodden to the bone, patched still with wilting white. The fields stretch dun and soaking, seams of white under every hedge-bank marking them out as though upon some strange and ancient map. The lanes are full of slush, splashing and dirty. The rivers run brown and galloping-high, licking at their banks and spilling over into the marshes. Near to the farmsteads the cattle stand hock-deep in the poached and oozing mud and the tractor-tracks are canyons in the squelch. The rain falls without ceasing.

It is a landscape of desolation. Yet there is a sweetness in the air, a proclamation that winter is passing. On the edge of a black and dripping wood the hazel bushes have put forth their pendant yellow catkins, and at the foot, see, a little knot of white that is not snow: the clustered heads of snowdrops. In a cottage garden by the moor, crocus, silken-coloured, thrust their buds above the wet wrack of winter. Somewhere a bird is singing. 'Spring's promise of Life.' So it is, so be it.

✳

137